People in Australia's Past

Stories & Activities

Second Edition

Susan Boyer

Boyer Educational Resources 2018

People in Australia's Past - Stories & Activities 2nd Edition   ISBN 978 1 877074 462
is proudly published in Australia by Boyer Educational Resources:
PO Box 255, Glenbrook, 2773, NSW, Australia,
Phone: 02 4739 1538 -- from outside Australia: + 61 2 4739 1538
Email: boyer@eftel.net.au   Web address: www.boyereducation.com.au

People in Australia's Past - Stories & Activities 2nd Edition   ISBN 978 1 877074 46 2
Also available:
People in Australia's Past - Audio CD (narration of the stories)   ISBN 978 1 877074 47 9
People in Australia's Past - Stories & Activities: Book & Audio CD   ISBN 978 1 877074 48 6

Cover design by Matt Thompson and Susan Boyer; Cover photography 'Outback road' by Len Boyer

Acknowledgments and further reading, see page 153.

Important cultural note:

Readers of **People in Australia's Past** please be aware that this book contains names and images of deceased persons, which in some Indigenous Australian communities may offend cultural prohibitions.

Teachers' note:

'People in Australia's Past' has been researched and developed by an English language and literacy teacher with a passion for Australian history.

The stories in this book relate to history topics of the **Australian Curriculum**, mid-upper primary school levels. See content descriptors taken directly from the Curriculum on the adjacent page or go to www.birrongbooks.com   for more detailed Australian Curriculum links.

The language activities in this book are suitable for teaching the interrelated strands of **language, literature and literacy** as specified in the Australian Curriculum, English.

As an additional resource to literacy teaching, **'People in Australia's Past' Audio CD** contains **narration of the twenty stories**. The audio narration, used concurrently with the written text can be a useful tool for developing literacy skills at all ages.

The stories and language activities have been carefully designed by teacher and author Susan Boyer for teaching **English as an Additional Language,** for adults as well as younger learners.

'People in Australia's Past' - 2nd Edition

Today Australia is a culturally diverse society but in global terms we are a young nation. Our multicultural history spans only a few centuries whereas Aboriginal peoples have lived on the Australian continent for thousands of years. This book begins with their story.

Also included are stories of individuals who have shaped Australia's history. Some, like **Mary Reibey** and **James Ruse** arrived as convicts with immense difficulties to overcome. On the other hand, women like **Elizabeth Macarthur**, **Elizabeth Macquarie** and **Caroline Chisholm** came as free settlers, and seeing problems in society, set out to bring change and progress.

Other history-makers were native born Australians like **David Unaipon**, **Edith Cowan**, **John Flynn**, **Eddie Mabo** and **Charles Perkins** who saw injustice and devoted their time and energy to bring progress in the fields of health, education and law reform. **Edmund Barton**, Australia's first Prime Minister, was a tireless advocate for the development of Australia's Constitution. In this 2nd edition, I have added the important stories of **Oodgeroo Noonuccal** and **Vincent Lingiari** who advanced the rights of Aboriginal Australians.

Some Australians gained fame through their discoveries or abilities. **Douglas Mawson** was an explorer who collected valuable scientific information in Antarctica. **Charles Kingsford Smith** set world records in flying across Australia and around the globe. **Banjo Paterson** is remembered for his unique stories of life in the Australian bush and for his celebrated song: 'Waltzing Matilda'. **Dame Nellie Melba** was Australia's first superstar, world famous for her beautiful voice.

Relevance to Australian Curriculum, English and History

As well as inspiring stories of people of diverse backgrounds, this resource provides material relating to the **Australian Curriculum**, **English** and **History.** For example, following each story are:

- topic related **vocabulary** activities involving matching words in the story to their meaning
- **comprehension activities** and varied **spelling** and **punctuation** activities
- **crosswords**, **map activities**, and **discussion** topics
- **models for writing information texts** (see biography template on page 121)

The stories relate to **History** topics of the **Australian Curriculum,** primary school levels:

Year 4 Level Description: How people, places and environments interact, past and present
Year 4 curriculum focuses on interactions between people, places and environments over time...

Year 4 Inquiry Question: What was life like for Aboriginal Peoples before the arrival of Europeans? How have laws affected the lives of people, past and present?

Year 5 Level Description: Australian communities – their past, present and possible futures
Year 5 curriculum focuses on colonial Australia in the 1800s and the social, economic, political and environmental causes and effects of Australia's development...

Year 5 Inquiry Question: How have individuals and groups in the past and present contributed to the development of Australia?

Year 6 Level Description: Australia in the past and present...
Year 6 curriculum focuses on the social, economic and political development of Australia as a nation, particularly after 1900, and Australia's role within a diverse and interconnected world.

Students explore the events and developments that shaped Australia as a democratic nation and stable economy, and the experiences of the diverse groups who have contributed to and are/were affected by these events and developments...

Year 6 Inquiry Question: How have key figures, events and values shaped Australian society, its system of government and citizenship?

** Language activities in this book are suitable for teaching **English as an Additional Language.**

People in Australia's Past – Contents

People in Australia's Past - Contents

Aboriginal Australians

The first residents of the Australian continent were the Aboriginal people. They understood the natural environment of Australia and lived in a sustainable way.

Aborigines lived in Australia for thousands of years before people arrived from Europe. They lived in tribes* and each tribal group had its own territory.

Before the European settlers arrived, there was nothing written about Aboriginal history. However, Aborigines taught their children about their history and culture through paintings on rocks and through dance, songs and stories called Dreamtime stories. Each story had a special message about the laws and customs of the tribe. The stories explained how the world began. They told the people how they must behave, how to find food and how to care for the land.

Aborigines lived on the land in a sustainable way. They believed they were part of nature, so they respected it and used only what they needed. They found enough food by moving between camps at different times of the year. Because they moved from place to place they didn't have many possessions. These things about Aboriginal culture were different from European culture. Europeans cut down trees, put up fences, built towns, collected possessions and believed that it was important to own the land.

When the British arrived in Australia, they decided the land wasn't owned by anyone because they saw no cities, fences or roads. At first, meetings between the British and Aboriginal people were careful but friendly. Aborigines were invited to live in the settlers' new town but most of them soon returned to their tribes and their own way of living. Many Aborigines were helpful to the settlers until they saw that the settlers were making farms where Aboriginal hunting and gathering places had always been. Soon there was not enough food left for them and they became hungry. However, when Aborigines went to the farms to pick the food growing there, they were chased away as thieves and many were killed. The Aboriginal people then killed white people in revenge and a clash of cultures began.

Aborigines had bush survival skills that the Europeans didn't know or understand. They knew how to find water in dry places and they could start a fire by rubbing sticks together. They had tools and weapons that were simple but very effective. They travelled from place to place without a compass or map. Many of the Europeans thought they were superior to the black natives and never tried to learn from them. As a result, many white people died when they got lost in the Australian bush.

Aboriginal culture is one of the oldest continuing cultures in the world and we can still learn from it. Answers to the problems of today's world, such as how to protect our natural environment and how to live in a sustainable way, were known and practised by Aborigines thousands of years ago.

*Some Aboriginal people use the term 'tribe' to describe their community, while others prefer the terms 'mob' or 'clan'.

'Two Aborigines spearing eels' by Joseph Lycett, 1817

A) Aboriginal Australians - Vocabulary activity

Find and highlight the following words in the story about Aboriginal Australians.
Write them next to their appropriate meaning. One has been done as an example.

continent	~~residents~~✓	tribes	sustainable	settlers	camps
thieves	respected	possessions	gathering		revenge
clash of cultures	effective	bush survival skills	superior	compass	

1) _____residents_____ - people who live in a particular place   Answers page, 122

2) _____ – a main area of land on the Earth, such as Africa, Asia, America, Australia

3) _____ – in ways that do not harm the environment but consider future needs

4) _____ - societies or family groups who share a community, culture and way of life

5) _____ - a group of people who move to a new place to live there

6) _____ - believed to be important and something to be cared for

7) _____ - places where people stay for a short time (sometimes in tents)

8) _____ - things that are owned by people, things that belong to people

9) _____ - collecting food and things that are needed

10) _____ - people who steal things from other people

11) _____ - hurt or harms someone because they had hurt someone you know

12) _____ - fight or disagree because ideas or cultures are different

13) _____ - skills that make it easy to live in the Australian bush

14) _____ - successful, does a job very well

15) _____ - something that shows which direction to go

16) _____ - better or in a higher position than others

B) Aboriginal Australians - Comprehension activity

Work in a group. One person should read aloud each question below.
Discuss the answer to each question together before you write anything.

1) Who were the first residents in Australia?

_____

2) How was the history of Aboriginal people told to their children?

_____

3) What were the Dreamtime stories about?

_____

_____

4) How did the Aborigines live on the land in a sustainable way?

_____

_____

5) How was Aboriginal culture different from European culture?

_____

6) When the British colony arrived what did they decide about the land and why?

_____

7) Why did Aborigines stop being helpful to the Europeans?

_____

8) What bush survival skills did the Aborigines have that were not known to the Europeans?

_____

_____

9) What problems of our modern world did Aborigines have answers for thousands of years ago?

_____

Answers: page 122

C) Language activities – English verbs review

Verbs are words that show what people **do**. Highlight the verbs in the following sentences:

I **run** often. They **bought** a new car. He **studies** everyday. He **eats** too many cakes.

There are two other very important English verbs. They are the verbs '**be**' and '**have**'.

'**be**' is the most common verb in English and is used in different ways depending on **who** and **when**. Look at the examples of the different forms of '**be**'. Highlight the verb in each sentence.

Past time	Present time	Future time
I was happy.	I am happy.	I will be happy.
She was happy.	She is happy.	She will be happy.
He was happy.	He is happy.	He will be happy.
You were happy.	You are happy.	You will be happy.
They were happy.	They are happy.	They will be happy.

'**have**' is another very common verb in English and is used in different ways.
Look at some examples of the different forms of '**have**'. Highlight the verb in each sentence.

Past time	Present time	Future time
I had a friend.	I have a friend.	I will have a friend.
She had a friend.	She has a friend.	She will have a friend.
He had a friend.	He has a friend.	He will have a friend.
You had a friend.	You have a friend.	You will have a friend.
They had a friend.	They have a friend.	They will have a friend.

<u>Tense</u> means <u>time period when something happens</u>. We talk about past tense, present tense, future tense.

We add '**d**' or '**ed**' to some verbs for past tense.

	Present	Past
For example:	walk ⟶	walk<u>ed</u>
	play ⟶	play<u>ed</u>

We change the spelling of some verbs for past tense.

	Present	Past
For example:	do ⟶	did
	see ⟶	saw

Complete the table with verbs from the text about Aboriginal Australians:

Past tense	Present tense
lived	_____
_____	move
_____	arrive
_____	believe
_____	need
_____	try *

* Verbs ending with the letter **y**; change **y** to **i** before -ed.

Past tense	Present tense
was	_____
_____	know
_____	think
_____	tell
_____	are
_____	have

Answers: page 122

Simple past tense verbs – crossword activity

a) Write the simple past tense of the verbs on the lines below. All the past tense verbs are in the story about Aboriginal Australians.

b) Write the **past tense verbs** next to the numbers in the crossword. One has been done as an example.

1. was	_____were_____	10. see	_____	19. can	_____
2. have	_____	11. become	_____	20. think	_____
3. live	_____	12. put	_____	21. invite	_____
4. begin	_____	13. tell	_____	22. chase	_____
5. build	_____	14. move	_____	23. decide	_____
6. own	_____	15. go	_____	24. cut	_____
7. arrive	_____	16. try	_____	25. is	_____
8. need	_____	17. find	_____	26. know	_____
9. understand	_____	18. use	_____		

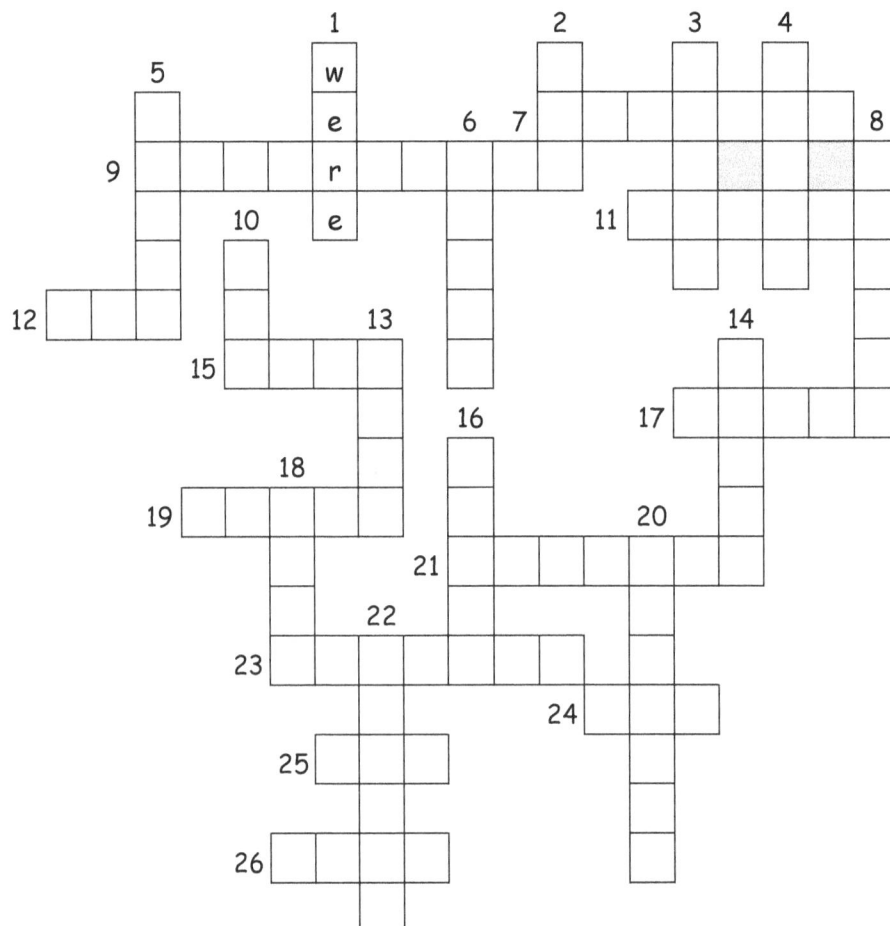

Answers: page 123

Aboriginal Australians

Put the verbs in the correct places in the story about Aboriginal Australians

lived (2 times)	taught	arrived	found	had (3 times)	moved
	chased	built	were (4 times)	owned	cut
saw (2 times)	went	began	thought	knew	tried	died

Aborigines _____ in Australia for thousands of years before people _____ from Europe. They _____ their children about their culture through paintings on rocks and through dance, songs and stories. Each story _____ a special message about the laws of the tribe and information about how to find food and how to care for the land.

Aborigines _____ in a sustainable way. They _____ enough food by moving between camps at different times of the year. Because they _____ from place to place they didn't have many possessions. These things about Aboriginal culture _____ different from European culture. Europeans _____ down trees, put up fences, _____ towns and believed that it was important to own the land.

When the British arrived in Australia, they decided the land wasn't _____ by anyone because they _____ no cities, fences or roads. At first, meetings between the British and Aboriginal people _____ careful but friendly. Many Aborigines _____ helpful to the settlers until they _____ the settlers were making farms where Aboriginal hunting and gathering places had always been. Soon there was not enough food left for them and they became hungry. However, when Aborigines _____ to the farms to pick the food growing there, they were _____ away as thieves and many were killed. The Aboriginal people then killed white people in revenge and a clash of cultures _____.

Aborigines _____ bush survival skills that the Europeans didn't know or understand. They _____ how to find water in dry places and they could start a fire by rubbing sticks together. They _____ tools and weapons that _____ simple but very effective. They moved from place to place to gather their food without compass or maps. Many of the Europeans _____ they were superior to the black people and never _____ to learn from them. As a result, many white people _____ when they got lost in the Australian bush.

Answers: page 123

Arthur Phillip

Arthur Phillip was the leader of the first British settlement in Australia. He was the first governor of the colony of New South Wales.

Arthur Phillip was born in London in 1738. He joined the British Navy when he was sixteen years old. During his time in the navy, he sailed to Spain, India, and South America. While he was not sailing with the navy, he lived on his farm in England.

In 1786, when he was 48, he was chosen as leader of the first fleet of eleven ships that would take hundreds of convicts to a place on the other side of the world. He would be the first governor of a new colony on the east coast of Australia. He was chosen for the job because he had experience in sailing, farming and in leading men. He would have complete authority over the new convict settlement.

Arthur Phillip spent many months planning for the voyage to the far side of the earth. He had to take everything a new colony may need. He had to take enough food for the long voyage and for the first year in the new place because they didn't know what food grew there.

Eleven ships left England in 1787 and arrived on the east coast of Australia on 26th January, 1788. The voyage of 12,000 miles had taken eight months and one week. Arthur Phillip found a place for the new settlement beside a good harbour. This place is now the world famous Sydney Harbour.

The real challenges began for Phillip the first day they arrived. There were more than a thousand people on the ships and more than 700 of them were convicts. When they landed, it was during the heat of summer but there were no houses or buildings to protect them from the hot or wet weather. There were no fields planted with vegetables or fruit. Many of the convicts were sick or weak from being on a ship for so long. Most of them were from cities and knew nothing about farming or building. The first years of the settlement were very difficult. There was a great food shortage so everyone, including Governor Phillip, had very little food. The ground around the settlement was too hard and dry to grow enough food and their equipment and tools were inadequate. Although there were many problems, Governor Phillip was an optimist.

He believed it was not necessary to lock up the convicts; they were on an island so it would be difficult for them to leave. Also, he needed workers to build the settlement. He decided the best idea was to get the convicts to work by offering them more freedom and the chance to farm their own piece of land if they behaved well.

By the time Arthur Phillip returned to England in 1792, Sydney had grown into a settlement of 4,000 people with buildings, roads and farms growing fresh food. He had laid the foundation for the nation of Australia. He imagined what was possible if people worked hard and worked together. Imagine if he could see Sydney today!

A) Arthur Phillip - Vocabulary activity

Find and highlight the following words and expressions in the story about Arthur Phillip. Write them next to their appropriate meaning. The first one has been done as an example.

governor	~~settlement~~ ✓	colony	authority	
fleet	voyage	harbour	convicts	landed	food shortage
challenges	an optimist	equipment	inadequate	imagine

1) _____settlement_____ – a new place or town built by people after arriving from another place

2) _____ – a person who governs a place that is controlled by another country

3) _____ - a place that is ruled and controlled by a far-away country

4) _____ – a group of ships traveling together

5) _____ - prisoners, people put in prison for doing bad things

6) _____ - the power to make decisions and control other people

7) _____ - a long trip to another place by ship

8) _____ - an area of water next to land where ships can be left safely

9) _____ - difficult situations; things that test people's ability

10) _____ - went on to the land after being on the water (sea, river or lake)

11) _____ - not enough food for people

12) _____ - tools or things needed and used to do a job

13) _____ - not good enough for a job or situation, not adequate

14) _____ - a positive person; someone who believes the best things are possible

15) _____ - to think about something, to have a picture or idea in your mind

Answers: page 124

B) Arthur Phillip - Comprehension activity

Work in a group. One person should read aloud each question below.
Discuss the answer to each question together before you write anything.

1) Who was Arthur Phillip?

_____

2) What job was he given when he was 48 years old?

_____

3) Why was he a good person for that job?

_____

4) What did he have to take on the voyage?

_____

5) How far was the voyage and how long did it take?

_____

6) What place did he choose for a settlement?

_____

7) How many people were part of the first settlement?

_____

8) What problems were there when they arrived?

_____   _____

_____   _____

_____   _____

9) What did Arthur Phillip decide to do with the convicts?

_____

10) What did Arthur Phillip do for Australia?

_____

Answers: page 124

See group speaking activities on pages 116 – 120.

See a biography writing activity on page 121.

10

C) Language activities – Paragraphs: grouping ideas in writing

When we write about a topic, we use sentences. Each sentence must have at least one verb.

Then we group the sentences together into **paragraphs**. Each paragraph starts on a new line and has at least one sentence. Each paragraph has a main topic or idea.

Look at the text about Arthur Phillip on page 8 again. How many paragraphs are there?
Write a number next to each paragraph on page 8 before you do the following activity.

Understanding the main idea of each paragraph

Choose the main idea of each paragraph.

The main idea of paragraph 1 is:

      a) where New South Wales is
      b) where Europe is
      c) who Arthur Phillip was

The main idea of paragraph 2 is:

      a) India
      b) Arthur Phillip's early life and career
      c) the ships

The main idea of paragraph 3 is:

      a) Phillip's farm
      b) Phillip was chosen to be leader of the first fleet
      c) Australia

The main idea of paragraph 4 is:

      a) the ships
      b) planning for the voyage
      c) the weather

The main idea of paragraph 5 is:

      a) the voyage
      b) Arthur Phillip's career
      c) the food

The main idea of paragraph 6 is:

      a) the challenges of the new settlement
      b) the journey to the new settlement
      c) the farms

The main idea of paragraph 7 is:

      a) Phillip's ideas for the convicts
      b) the weather
      c) Aborigines

The main idea of paragraph 8 is:

      a) the results of Arthur Phillip's work
      b) the plants and vegetables
      c) where Sydney is

Answers: page 124

Nouns

You can see in the box below the names of things brought to Australia on the ships of the First Fleet. All the words in the box are nouns. Nouns are the **names** of things.

Write the names of the things in the pictures on the lines below.   Answers: page 125

Equipment brought to Australia on the First Fleet of 1788.

~~candles~~	hatchet	rope	tents	hammer and nails	fish hooks
cooking pot	handsaw		hinges	wheelbarrow	shovel
cart	cotton thread		handcuffs	padlocks	axe
hoe		carriage		pickaxe	hammock

1 candles

2 _____

3 _____

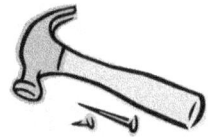

4 _____

5. _____

6 _____

7 _____

8 _____

9 _____

10 _____

11 _____

12 _____

13 _____

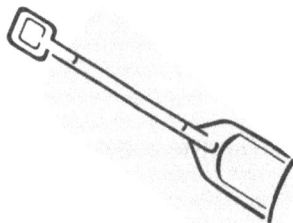

14 _____

15 _____

16 _____

17 _____

18 _____

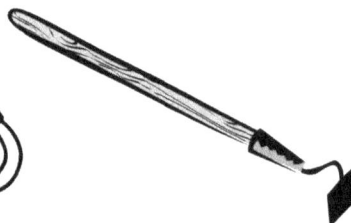

19 _____

20 _____

Crossword – tools and equipment

Write the nouns from page 12 next to numbers in the crossword. One has been done as an example.

```
                1                              2
                c           3
            4   a                   ▓       ▓
                n
                d
                l         5
        6       e
    7           s                       8   9
                            10      11
    12
        13              ▓               14
    15              ▓                   16
            17
18                              19
                        20
```

Answers: page 125

What would you take?

If you were leader of the First Fleet in 1788 what equipment and supplies would **you** take on the ships?
Write things under each heading below, using the nouns on page 14 as well as adding other things.

Food (including seeds and animals)	Clothes
Tools and equipment	**Furniture and housing**

Compare your list with the 'First Fleet Equipment List' at: www.birrongbooks.com

Click on 'Free Resources - Stories of Life at Sydney Cove' for a free PDF download.

Conjunctions - Joining different pieces of information in sentences

Some sentences contain only one idea or piece of information.
For example: The first years of the settlement were very difficult.

Some sentences contain two or more pieces of information.

We join ideas in sentences by using **joining words** which we call **conjunctions** or **connectives**.
Conjunctions are words such as: and, but, because, that, when, while, so, if, however.

Add connectives to the following sentences from the story about Arthur Phillip.
You can check '**How we use conjunctions**' at the bottom of this page if necessary.

and	when	while	but	or	because	if (2 times)	so (2 times)	although

1) He joined the British Navy _____ he was sixteen years old.

2) _____ he was not sailing with the navy, he lived on his farm in England.

3) He was chosen for the job _____ he had experience in sailing, farming and in leading men.

4) When they landed, it was during the heat of summer _____ there were no houses _____ buildings to protect them from the hot weather.

5) There was a great food shortage _____ everyone, including Governor Phillip, had very little food.

6) _____ there were many problems, Governor Phillip was an optimist!

7) They were on an island _____ it would be difficult for them to leave.

8) He decided the best idea was to get the convicts to work by offering them more freedom _____ the chance to farm their own piece of land _____ they behaved well.

9) He imagined what was possible _____ people worked hard and worked together.

You can check your answers by reading the story about Arthur Phillip again or see page 125.

How we use conjunctions
- **and** connects similar ideas or things
- **when** and **while** connect an event and the time or time period of another event
- **so** and **because** are used to connect a reason for an action
- **however**, **although** and **but** are used to join different or opposite ideas or situations
- **or** connects choices or different possibilities
- **if** is used to say something is possible in a particular situation

Map Activity

The map shows where the 'First Fleet' travelled from England to New South Wales and where they stopped. Write the place names on the map of the world. You can use an atlas to help you.

England	~~Tenerife~~ ✓	Rio de Janeiro	South America
Cape of Good Hope		Africa	Australia

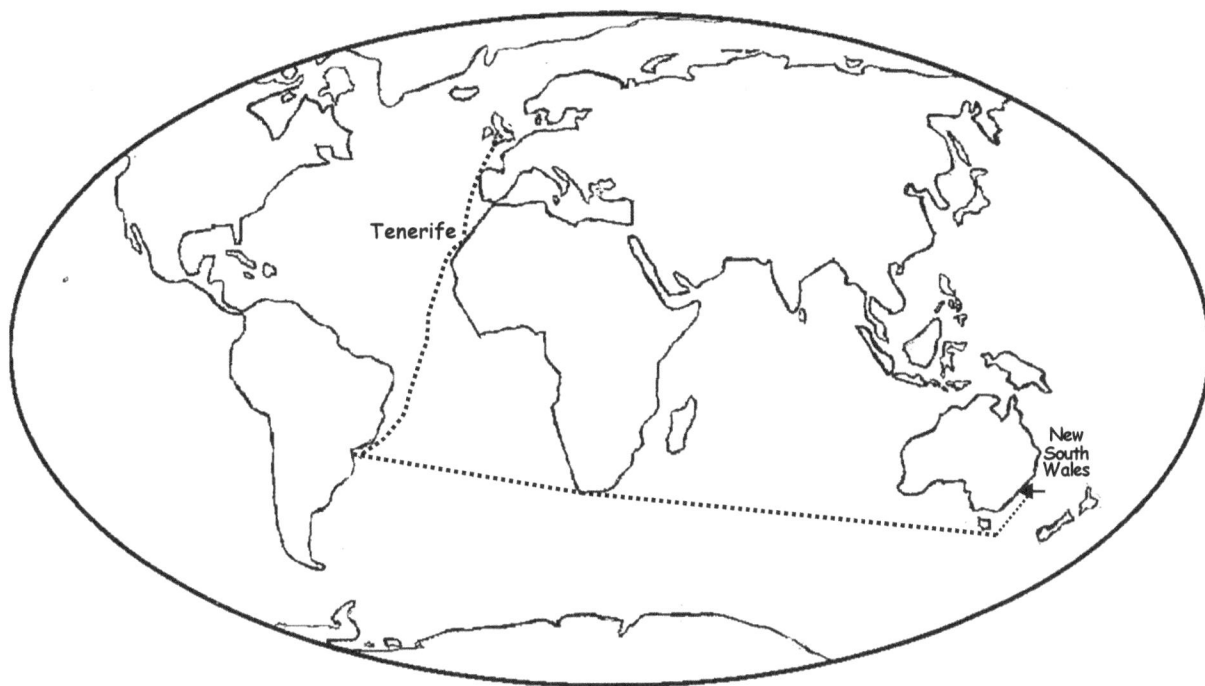

Tenerife

New South Wales

Answers: page 125

Discuss & write – Convicts of the 'First Fleet'

Write a list of the **jobs** that would need to be done when the convicts of the 'First Fleet' arrived in New South Wales to establish a colony.

_____

_____

_____

_____

_____

_____

Bennelong

Bennelong was an Aboriginal man who became a mediator between Aboriginal and European cultures. He tried to build friendship between his people and the settlers of the First Fleet. He learnt to speak English and explained many things about his culture to the new white settlers.

As soon as the First Fleet arrived in Sydney, Governor Phillip tried to build friendship with the Aboriginal people. However, the Aborigines were shocked to see the British cutting down trees, taking over their hunting and fishing places and building houses and fences. They were shocked to see convicts being beaten by soldiers and working in chains so they stayed away from the British settlement. Governor Phillip was worried about this so he decided to kidnap some Aborigines to show them the benefits of living as a European.

A few days later, Bennelong was grabbed on a beach and taken to Governor Phillip's house as a prisoner, although he had done nothing wrong. He was about 25 years old at the time. Of course, this was not a good way to begin a friendship and at first Bennelong was very afraid and angry. However, he soon saw that he was being treated well and eventually a friendship began between him and Governor Phillip.

After some time, Bennelong began calling the Governor by an Aboriginal word which meant 'father' and Phillip called Bennelong by an Aboriginal name meaning 'son'. Bennelong lived and ate well in the Governor's house. He learnt English and wore European clothes. He drank wine and made jokes with the officers. However, he was not free to leave whenever he wished and he missed his freedom and his own cultural ways. The following year, he escaped in the middle of the night and went back to his people.

Nobody from the British settlement saw Bennelong for several months, until one day he met the Governor and some officers on a beach on the far side of the harbour. Governor Phillip promised Bennelong that if he returned to the Sydney settlement, he would have complete freedom to return to his people whenever he wished. Bennelong agreed to this and began visiting the settlement often, bringing other Aborigines with him. Governor Phillip had a small house built for Bennelong near the main Sydney settlement, where he spent a lot of time as a mediator between the black and white cultures. Today this place is called Bennelong Point and is the place where the Sydney Opera House now stands.

When Governor Phillip returned to England in 1792, Bennelong and another Aboriginal man decided to go with him. However, both Aboriginal men had problems living in the cold English climate and became very homesick. Bennelong began drinking too much alcohol and became sick and depressed by the time he returned to Australia three years later. Sadly, his bad health continued until his death in 1813.

Bennelong was an intelligent, good-humoured and open-minded man, who tried to improve the relationship between his culture and one that was very different to his. He is remembered today as one of Australia's first diplomats.

A) Bennelong - Vocabulary activity

Find and highlights the following words and expressions in the story about Bennelong.
Write them next to the appropriate meaning. The first one has been done as an example.

beaten	mediator ✓	kidnap	taking over	shocked	in chains
grabbed	eventually	escaped	made jokes	homesick	depressed
climate	good-humoured	diplomats	open-minded	intelligent

1. _____mediator_____ - a person who helps to make peace between two groups of people

2. _____ - had a sudden bad feeling because of something seen or heard

3. _____ - start using and controlling something that belongs to other people

4. _____ - being hit many times by another person

5. _____ - metal pieces around the legs to stop a prisoner from running

6. _____ - take someone away from their home and keep them as a prisoner

7. _____ - to be caught and taken hold of by someone suddenly

8. _____ - after some time has gone by

9. _____ - told funny stories to make people laugh

10. _____ - left or got away from a place or situation that he didn't like

11. _____ - the weather conditions

12. _____ - feeling sad because you are away from your home and family

13. _____ - a feeling of being very unhappy

14. _____ - clever

15. _____ _____ - happy and friendly

16. _____ _____ - happy to listen to ideas or opinions that are new or different to yours

17. _____ - people who keep good and peaceful relations between two nations

Answers: page 126

B) Bennelong - Comprehension activity

Work in a group. One person should read aloud each question below.
Discuss the answer to each question together before you write anything.

1) Who was Bennelong?

_____

2) Why did the Aborigines stay away from the British settlers after they first arrived?

_____

_____

3) What did Governor Phillip do to Bennelong?

_____

4) What happened when Bennelong lived in Governor Phillip's house?

_____

_____

5) Why did he escape?

_____

6) What did Governor Phillip promise to Bennelong if he returned to Sydney?

_____

7) Where did Bennelong go in 1792?

_____

8) What happened to Bennelong in England?

_____

9) What kind of man was Bennelong?

_____

10) How is Bennelong remembered today?

_____

Answers: page 126

See group speaking activities on pages 116 - 120.

See a biography writing activity on page 121.

C) Language activities: Grammar - nouns

Nouns are the names of people, places, things, feelings and conditions.

Proper nouns are specific names for people, places, days, months and special events.
The names of countries, nationalities, cities and languages are proper nouns.
All **proper nouns** begin with a **capital letter**.

Write examples of proper nouns from the 'Bennelong' story:

People	Places	Nationalities
__Bennelong__	__England__	__European__
_____	_____	_____

Common nouns are the general names of people, things, conditions or experiences.

Look at examples of two categories of common nouns:

concrete nouns names of people, places or things we can see or touch	abstract nouns names of experiences, feelings or conditions that can't be seen or touched
soldier road house	language happiness peace

Write these nouns from the '**Bennelong**' text in the correct column below.

~~harbour~~ ✓	~~mediator~~ ✓	~~trees~~ ✓	~~culture~~ ✓	diplomat	friendship	settlers	houses
convicts	chains	beach	prisoner	freedom	father	son	man
clothes	time	fences	officers	settlement	problems	climate	health

concrete nouns			abstract nouns
places	people	things	conditions, experiences and feelings
harbour	mediator	trees	culture

Answers: page 126

James Ruse

James Ruse was a pioneer farmer in Australia. He was the first convict in Australia to be given land for farming and to be self-sufficient by producing his own food from a small piece of land.

James Ruse was born on a farm in England in 1759.
When he was 23 years old, he was arrested for stealing two silver watches. For punishment, he was sent as a convict to work for seven years in the colony in Sydney, New South Wales. He travelled on one of the ships of the First Fleet that arrived in Australia in January, 1788.

Soon after the people of the First Fleet arrived in Sydney there were problems. Governor Phillip knew the food they'd brought with them from England would soon be gone. He knew they must grow their own food or they would starve. But the land around Sydney was hard and not good for growing vegetables. The seasons were different to Europe. The weather was very hot and many things were new and unfamiliar. Some of the convicts were sick and weak. Many of them were lazy and not interested in trying to grow anything.

James Ruse was different; he wanted to give it a go. He told Governor Phillip that he had experience as a farmer. He asked if he could have some land to grow food and show that he could become self-sufficient in a short time. Governor Phillip allowed James to live and work on a small area of land near the Parramatta River, twenty kilometres west of Sydney. Governor Phillip allowed this because he saw that James Ruse was a well-behaved convict. It was an experiment to see if it was possible to succeed in farming in a country where the seasons and soil were unfamiliar. James Ruse's farm was called 'Experiment Farm'.

James and his wife Elizabeth were given clothes, tools, chickens and some vegetable seeds, as well as help to clear and dig the land. They worked hard and after only fifteen months they could say they were successful. They showed that it was possible for a family to survive through farming in the colony of New South Wales. Governor Phillip was very pleased because the success of James and his wife made other convicts want to try the same methods. Within a few months, a farming community began near the Parramatta River.

As a reward for his hard work, Governor Phillip allowed James to keep his farm. This meant that although James was still a convict, he would become the owner of his own piece of land. This happened in 1791 and was the first land grant to a convict in Australia.

James and Elizabeth had three children, and later sold their first farm and moved on to build a bigger and more successful one. Later they had problems such as droughts and floods, however, they showed that successful farming was possible in Australia and they never returned to England. They showed that hard work and being ready to try new methods in an unfamiliar place could bring success, even when other people didn't believe it was possible.

A) James Ruse - Vocabulary activity

Find and highlight the following words and expressions in the story about James Ruse.
Write them next to their appropriate meaning. The first one has been done as an example.

colony	~~pioneer~~✓	self-sufficient	seasons	punishment	arrested
First Fleet	starve	unfamiliar	experiment	well-behaved	survive
	give it a go	methods	land grant	droughts	

1) _____pioneer_____ – the first person to do something and then show other people the way

2) _____ - having everything necessary to live, to be independent

3) _____ - caught and asked questions by police about a crime, may be put in prison

4) _____ - when a person is made to suffer because they did something bad

5) _____ - a place that is ruled and controlled by a far-away country

6) _____ - the first group of 11 ships to arrive in Sydney with convicts

7) _____ - die from hunger, not have enough food to keep living

8) _____ - parts of the year: summer, winter, autumn, spring

9) _____ - different, not understood or not known before

10) _____ - try to do something

11) _____ - being good and doing the right thing

12) _____ - a test to see if something is possible and to see if it will succeed

13) _____ - continue to live through a difficult situation

14) _____ - ways of doing something

15) _____ - land given to someone by the government

16) _____ - long periods of time without rain, when there is not enough water

Answers: page 127

B) James Ruse - Comprehension activity

Work in a group. One person should read aloud each question below.
Discuss the answer to each question together before you write anything.

1) Who was James Ruse?

_____

2) What happened when James was 23 years old?

_____

3) What was his punishment?

_____

4) What problems did the people of the First Fleet have when they arrived in New South Wales?

_____

_____

5) How was James Ruse different to many of the other convicts?

_____

6) Why did Governor Phillip allow James to live and work on a farm near the Parramatta River?

_____

_____

7) What help was James and his wife, Elizabeth given?

_____

8) Why was Governor Phillip pleased with the result?

_____

9) What reward was James given?

_____

10) What did James and his wife show was possible?

_____

Answers: page 127

See group speaking activities on pages 116 – 120.

See a biography writing activity on page 121.

C) Language activities – Nouns revision

Nouns are the names of people, places, things, feelings and conditions.

Put the nouns in the correct places in the 'James Ruse' story. One has been done as an example.

land (2 times)	~~farmer~~ ✓	convict	problems	food	watches	punishment
colony	years	ships	experience	Australia	kilometres	clothes
wife	chickens	seeds	farm	months	family	
work	droughts	reward				

James Ruse was a pioneer _farmer_ in Australia. He was the first

_____ in Australia to be given _____ for farming.

James Ruse was born on a farm in England in 1759. When he was 23,

police arrested him for stealing two silver _____. For _____,

he was sent to work for seven _____ in the _____ of New South Wales. He travelled

on one of the _____ of the First Fleet that arrived in Australia in 1788.

Soon after the First Fleet arrived in Sydney, there were _____. The food they'd brought

with them from England would soon be gone and Governor Phillip knew that they must grow their

own _____ or they would starve.

James Ruse told Governor Phillip that he had _____ as a farmer. He asked if he could

have some _____ to grow food and show that he could become self-sufficient in a short period

of time. Governor Phillip allowed James to live and work on land near the Parramatta River, twenty

_____ west of Sydney.

James and his _____ Elizabeth were given _____, tools, _____ and some

vegetable _____, as well as help to clear and dig more land. They worked hard and after

only fifteen _____ they could say they were successful. They showed that it was possible

for a _____ to survive through farming in the colony of New South Wales.

As a _____ for his hard work, Governor Phillip allowed James to keep his farm. This happened

in 1791 and was the first land grant to a convict in _____. James and Elizabeth had

three children, and later sold their first _____ and moved on to build a much bigger one.

Later they had problems such as _____ and floods, however, they showed that hard

_____ could bring success, even when other people didn't believe it was possible.

Answers: page 127

Adjectives and Nouns

Adjectives are words that <u>describe</u> nouns. (people, places, things and conditions).
Adjectives give more information about the nouns in sentences.
<u>Underline</u> the words that <u>describe</u> something in the following sentences:

The weather was hot.
The ground was hard.

The following box contains nouns and adjectives from the story about James Ruse.
Write the words in the correct column. Answers: page 128.

~~farmer~~ ✓	~~interested~~ ✓	vegetables	different	sick	weak	unfamiliar
bigger	watches	successful	silver	tools	lazy	soil
clothes	convicts	food	colony	same		

nouns	adjectives
farmer	interested

Put the adjectives below in the correct places in the story about James Ruse.

| sick | ~~hard~~ ✓ | new | different | lazy | weak | interested | small |
| self-sufficient | successful | well-behaved | hot | short | first | unfamiliar | |

Soon after the people of the First Fleet arrived in Sydney there were problems. The food they'd brought with them from England would soon be gone. But the land around Sydney was <u>**hard**</u> [1] and not good for growing vegetables. The weather was very _____ [2] and many things were _____ [3] and unfamiliar. Some of the convicts were _____ [4] and _____ [5]. Many of them were _____ [6] and not _____ [7] in trying to grow anything.

James Ruse was _____ [8]; he wanted to give it a go. He told Governor Phillip that he had experience as a farmer. He asked if he could have some land to grow food and show that he could become _____-_____ [9] in a _____ [10] time. Governor Phillip allowed James to live and work on a _____ [11] area of land near the Parramatta River. Governor Phillip allowed this because he saw that James Ruse was a _____-_____ [12] convict. It was an experiment to see if it was possible to succeed in farming in a country where the seasons and the soil were _____ [13]. James Ruse's farm was called 'Experiment Farm'.

James and Elizabeth had three children, and later sold their_____ [14] farm and moved on to build a bigger and more _____ [15] one.

Answers: page 128

Adjectives- spelling practice

Write adjectives from the story about James Ruse (page 24) into the crossword next to the corresponding numbers. One has been done as an example.

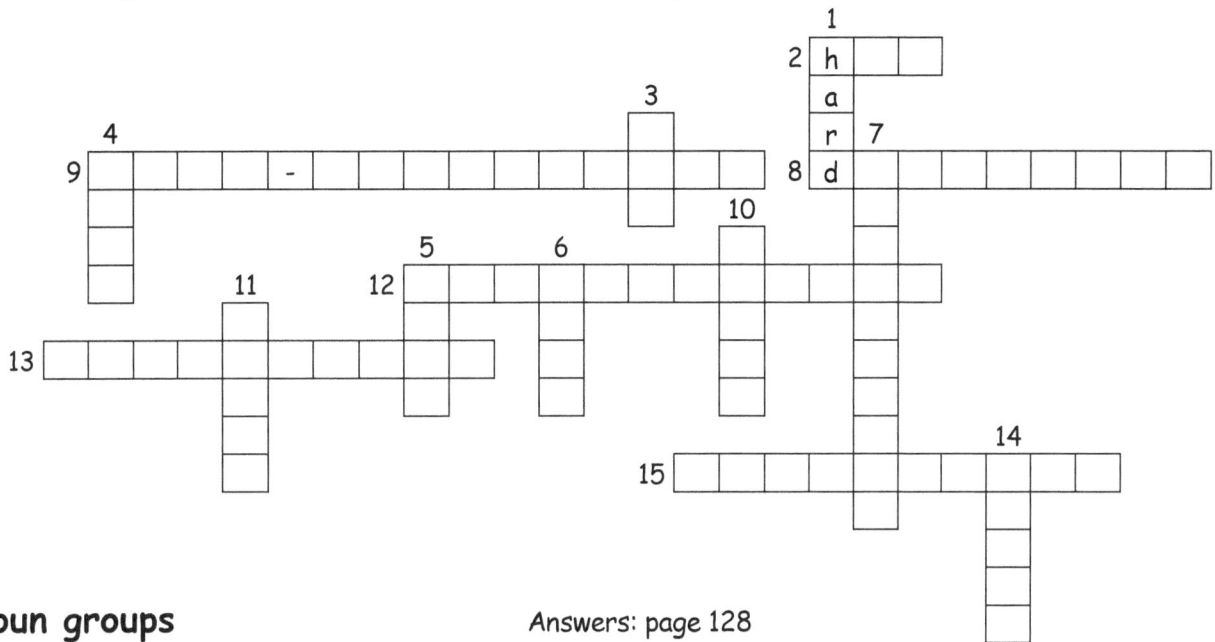

Noun groups

Answers: page 128

A noun group is a group of words that describes a person, place or thing; it includes one or more nouns and often includes one or more adjectives. In stories, noun groups help the reader imagine the people and situations. Noun groups tell us <u>who</u>, <u>what</u> or <u>where</u>.

Look at the following question and answer. The noun group in the answer is <u>underlined</u>.

Question: Who was Arthur Phillip?
Answer: Arthur Phillip was <u>the first governor of the colony of New South Wales</u>.

The noun group gives information about <u>who</u> Arthur Phillip was; it describes him.

Practice

Underline the noun group in each sentence below to answer the questions about James Ruse.

Questions:	Answers (see page 128)
1) Where was James Ruse born? →	James Ruse was born on <u>a farm in England</u>.
2) Who was James Ruse?	James Ruse was a pioneer farmer in Australia.
3) What did James Ruse steal?	He stole two silver watches.
4) What kind of convict was James Ruse?	James Ruse was a well-behaved convict.
5) What did James Ruse live and work on?	James Ruse lived and worked on a small area of land near the Parramatta River.
6) What was James given?	In 1791, James was given the first convict land grant in Australia.
7) What did James finally own?	James became the owner of his own piece of land.
8) What did he build after he sold his first farm?	James later sold his first farm and built a bigger and more successful one.

Mary Reibey

Mary Reibey was an English girl who was sent to Australia as a convict when she was only thirteen years old. Later she became one of Sydney's most successful businesswomen.

Mary was born in England in 1777. Her parents died when she was a young girl so she lived with her grandmother. When she was 13 years old, police arrested her for trying to steal a horse. When the police arrested her, she was dressed as a boy and she said her name was James Burrow. For punishment, she was sent as a convict to work for seven years in the new colony in Sydney, New South Wales.

She was taken to Australia by ship and when she arrived in 1792, she was given a job looking after small children in a home. When she was seventeen, she married Thomas Reibey, a young Irish officer she had met on the ship while coming to Australia. After their marriage, Thomas and Mary lived on a farm along the Hawkesbury River, north of Sydney. Soon they started a business delivering things by boat to people who lived along the river. By 1803 they owned three boats and expanded their business to deliver food and other supplies to settlers who lived further from Sydney along the coast. In 1807 Thomas bought a larger sailing ship for trading with the Pacific Islands, China and India. However he became very sick after a trip to India in 1809.

When he died in 1811, Mary was left with seven children and a very large business to manage alone. But she continued because she had perseverance and was determined to be successful. It was not easy for her, because it was unusual for a woman to manage a large business at that time in history. However, the following year, in 1812, Mary opened a new warehouse in George Street, Sydney and in 1817 she bought two more ships. During the next ten years, her business continued to grow and she built many large buildings in the business centre of Sydney.

Mary was a determined, hard working person who showed that it was possible to be successful, even though her younger life had been very difficult. Even when she retired, she was interested in helping other people and gave money to support a free school in Sydney. She died in 1855, at the age of 78.

Because of her hard work and perseverance, Mary became one of the most successful and respected businesswomen in the early history of Australia. You can see a picture of Mary Reibey, a sailing ship and one of her Sydney buildings on the Australian twenty dollar note.

A) Mary Reibey - Vocabulary activity

Find and highlight the following words and expressions in the story about Mary Reibey.
Write them next to the appropriate meaning. The first one has been done as an example.

convict	~~arrested~~ ✓	officer	colony	punishment	delivering
supplies		trading	perseverance		determined
	warehouse	retired	respected		

1. _____arrested_____ - caught and asked questions by police about a crime, maybe put in prison

2. _____ - something done to a person because they did something bad

3. _____ - a person who is put in prison for doing something bad

4. _____ - a place that is ruled and controlled by a far-away country

5. _____ - a person with an important job in the army or navy

6. _____ - taking things to a person or a place

7. _____ - the things that people need and use to live and work

8. _____ - buying and selling between people or countries

9. _____ - continuing to try and do something when things are very difficult

10. _____ - wanting to do something very much and not letting anything stop you

11. _____ - a very large building where things are stored before they are used or sold

12. _____ - stopped working because of old age

13. _____ – approved and admired by other people for their good work

Answers: page 129

This painting was by John Carmichael, 1829. Its title is 'George Street from the Wharf'.
Mary's townhouse was on George Street. You can see the building on the $20 note.

B) Mary Reibey - Comprehension activity

Work in a group. One person should read aloud each question below.
Discuss the answer to each question together before you write anything.

1) Where and when was Mary Reibey born?

_____

 2) What happened when Mary was 13 years old?

_____

_____

3) Who did she marry?

_____

4) What kind of business did they start?

_____

5) What did they buy in 1807?

_____

6) What happened in 1811?

_____

7) What did Mary do after her husband died?

_____

_____

8) What did other people in the colony think about Mary Reibey?

_____

9) What can we see on the $20 note?

_____

Answers: page 129

Discuss – Crime and Punishment

1. What did Mary do to receive the punishment of being sent to New South Wales as a convict?

2. Do you think the punishment she received was fair?

3. If someone did the same thing now, what punishment do you think they would get?

4. Do you think the types of punishment that people get now are fair?

C) Language activities – more practice with nouns

Nouns (names of things) can be divided into categories: proper nouns and common nouns.

Proper nouns are specific names for people, places, nationalities, days, months and special events. Proper nouns always begin with a capital letter. For example: <u>M</u>ary <u>R</u>eibey was <u>E</u>nglish.

Write more examples of proper nouns from the 'Mary Reibey' story:

People	Places	Nationalities
Mary Reibey	China	English
_____	_____	_____

Common nouns are the general names of places, people, things and conditions or experiences.

Look at examples of two categories of common nouns:

concrete nouns: names of people, places or things we can see or touch	**abstract nouns**: names of experiences, feelings or conditions that we can't see or touch
girl river horse	success life perseverance

Write the following nouns from the '**Mary Reibey**' story in the correct columns below.

convict	marriage	picture	girl	grandmother	islands
police	boy	age	punishment	colony	ship
history	farm	children	officer	perseverance	boat

concrete nouns			abstract nouns
places	people	things	conditions, experiences and feelings
colony	girl	ship	perseverance

Answers: page 129

Verbs and nouns with the same spelling

Some English words can be used as verbs or nouns in sentences. The meaning of the word depends on how it is used in the sentence; it depends on the context.

Look at these examples:
      verb
      I <u>help</u> my friend every week.   noun
      I need <u>help</u> with my homework.

Read the sentences below and write *verb* or *noun* above the <u>underlined</u> words as in the example above.

Mary lived on a <u>farm</u>.   Mary can <u>farm</u> vegetables and animals.

Look at Mary's <u>picture</u> on the $20.   Can you <u>picture</u> life on a convict ship?

Mary was arrested by the <u>police</u>.   They <u>police</u> the area after rock concerts.

I <u>work</u> six days each week.   My <u>work</u> is very enjoyable.

What is your <u>age</u>?   Your skin will <u>age</u> quickly without sunscreen.

Nouns review - Mary Reibey

Put the nouns in the correct places in the story about Mary Reibey.

convict	years	picture	police	horse	boy	colony
Australia		ship (2 times)		business (2 times)		river
work	children (2 times)		warehouse		buildings (2 times)	

Mary Reibey was an English girl who was sent to Australia

as a _____ when she was only 13 _____ old.

Later she became one of Sydney's most successful businesswomen.

When she was 13 years old, _____ arrested her for trying to steal a _____.

When the police arrested her, she was dressed as a _____ and she said her name was James

Burrow. For punishment, she was sent as a convict to work for seven years in the new

_____ in Sydney, New South Wales.

She was taken to _____ by _____ and when she arrived in 1792, she was

given a job looking after small _____ in a home. When she was seventeen, she married

Thomas Reibey. Soon they started a _____ delivering things by boat to people who

lived along the _____. In 1807 Thomas bought a larger sailing ship for trading with the

Pacific Islands, China and India, but he became sick after a trip to India in 1809.

Thomas died in 1811 and Mary was left with seven _____ and a very large _____

to manage alone. However, the next year, in 1812, Mary opened a new _____ in

Sydney and bought two more ships in 1817. During the next ten years, her business continued to

grow and she built many large _____ in the business centre of Sydney.

Because of her hard _____, Mary Reibey became one of the most successful

businesswomen in the early history of New South Wales.

You can see a _____ of Mary,

a sailing _____ and one of her Sydney

_____ on the Australian twenty

dollar note.

Answers: page 130

Map Activity

Complete the following sentence about Mary Reibey with the place names below:

Mary was born in _____ in 1777. She was taken to _____ by ship in 1792. Mary and Thomas Reibey bought ships to trade with the Pacific Islands, _____ and _____.

Check the following places in an atlas, then show them on the world map below:

Pacific Ocean

Australia

England

China

India

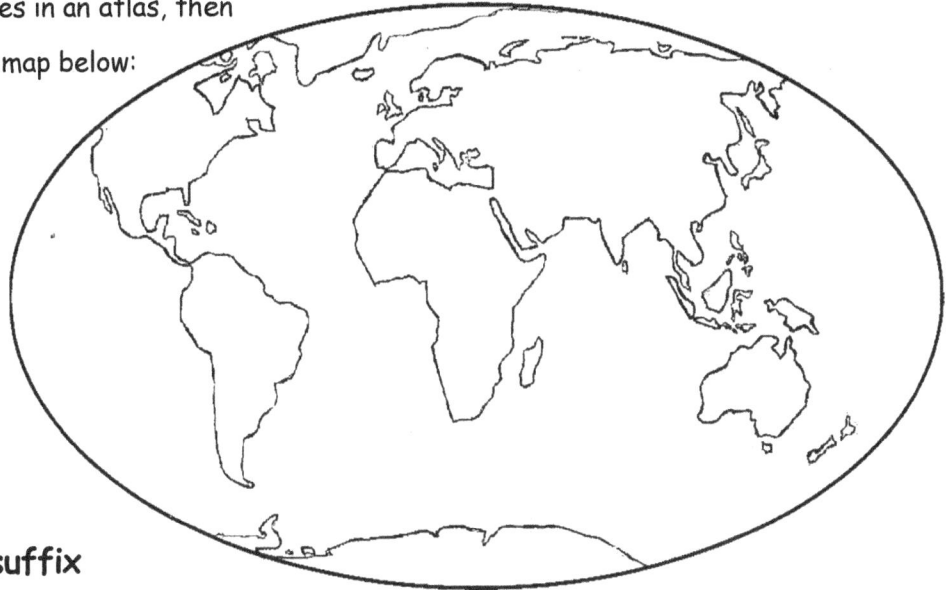

Adjectives with a suffix

Some English nouns can be made into adjectives by adding a suffix.
A suffix is a group of letters added to the end of a word to change the meaning.

For example, to change the noun 'success' to an adjective (successful), we add the suffix 'ful'.
Adjectives ending with 'ful', describe a person or thing which 'has or gives a particular quality'.
For example, we can say 'Mary had success in New South Wales' or 'Mary was successful'.

Usually, if a noun ends with 'y', we change **y** to **i**, before adding ful, eg. beauty → beautiful.

Write adjectives next to the following nouns, by adding the suffix 'ful'.

1) care ____careful____   2) help _____   3) power _____

4) success _____   5) hope _____   6) respect _____

7) beauty _____   8) skill _____   9) truth _____

10) law _____

Write the adjectives in the crossword, next to the numbers.

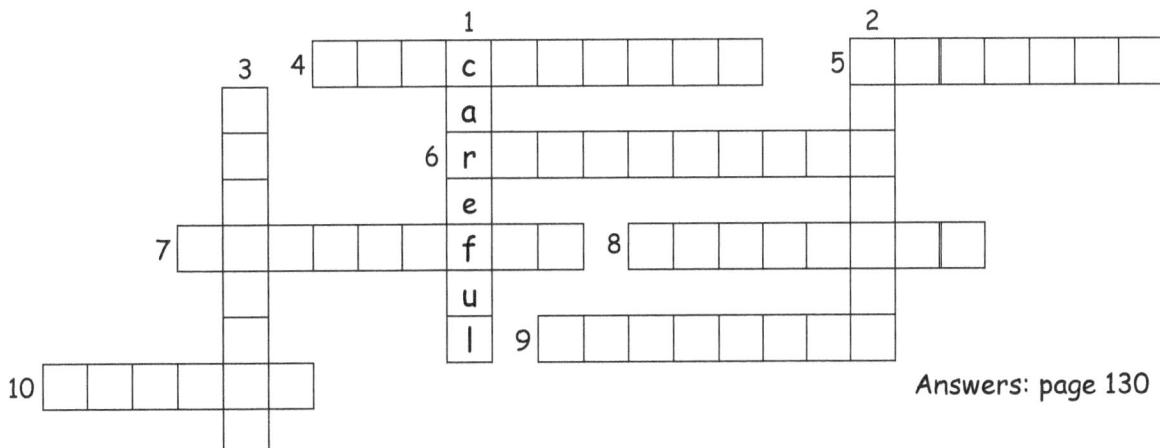

Answers: page 130

John and Elizabeth Macarthur

John and Elizabeth Macarthur are known as the founders of the Australian wool industry.

John and Elizabeth married in England in 1788. The next year, they sailed with their baby son, Edward, to the colony of New South Wales. John was sent to the colony as a soldier in the New South Wales Corps which was a special army sent to control the convict colony.

John Macarthur was a clever, ambitious man. He was soon put in charge of a farming settlement at Parramatta, where he had a large farm which he named 'Elizabeth Farm'. He was given the job of paymaster to the army and inspector of all public work in the colony, such as new buildings and roads. These jobs gave him a lot of power and control. He used convict workers and government equipment on his farm and then he sold the produce from the farm to the government for a profit.

In 1795, John and Elizabeth began experimenting with sheep farming because they thought it would make more profit than growing vegetables. Soon after, they bought some Merino sheep which came from Spain. They thought Merinos would do well in Australia's hot, dry climate which was similar to the climate of Spain. Later, Macarthur quit his job in the army to spend more time on his farming and business interests.

During his time in the colony, John Macarthur made a lot of enemies. He fought with his neighbours and argued with the governors of the colony and then tried to use his friendship with powerful people in England to make trouble for anyone who disagreed with him. In 1801, Governor King sent Macarthur back to England to face court over his serious troublemaking.

John was away from Australia for almost four years. Meanwhile, Elizabeth had to look after their young children, as well as the farm. This included management of the house and business accounts, management of convict workers, the shearing of sheep and selling of wool, as well as the transport and buying of new sheep. All this time she continued to improve 'Elizabeth Farm' and produce Merino sheep with better wool.

While John was in England, he used the opportunity to show his samples of wool to people in the British wool industry. He had a lot of support from important people in England and when he returned to Australia he was given more of the best land in the colony to continue sheep farming.

In 1809, after getting into more trouble with the government, John left Australia to go to Europe. This time he was away for seven years and Elizabeth was again left to manage their large sheep farm. John Macarthur was only allowed to return to the colony in 1817 after promising he would stay out of trouble. Back in Australia, he gave his full attention to developing the wool industry. John and Elizabeth, with the help of their sons, were soon exporting wool to England and continued to expand their business.

With hard work and determination they established the Australian wool industry. Today Australia is the world's largest producer of wool.

A) John and Elizabeth Macarthur - Vocabulary activity

Find the following words and expressions in the story about John and Elizabeth Macarthur. Write them next to the appropriate meaning below. The first one has been done as an example.

ambitious	~~founders~~ ✓	profit	in charge	inspector	produce
	experimenting	argued	troublemaking		enemies
samples	opportunity	support	expand	exporting	determination

1. _____founders_____ - people who begin a new activity or an organisation

2._____ - a strong feeling of wanting to be successful

3. _____ - to be in control of a job or other people

4._____ - someone whose job is to check that things are done correctly

5._____ - food that is grown on a farm to be sold

6._____ - money that is made from selling something

7._____ - trying or testing a new way of doing something

8._____ - people who hate each other and fight each other

9._____ - disagreed with another person, shouted in an angry way

10._____ - making problems for other people

11._____ - a good situation which gives you a chance to do something

12._____ - small examples or pieces of something to show as examples

13._____ - help

14._____ - sending and selling produce to another country

15._____ - to get bigger, increase in size and number

16._____ - a strong feeling of wanting to do something very much and not letting anything stop you

Answers: page 131

B) John and Elizabeth Macarthur - Comprehension activity

Work in a group. One person should read aloud each question below.
Discuss the answer to each question together before you write anything.

1) Why are John and Elizabeth Macarthur remembered?

_____

2) Why did John Macarthur travel to Australia?

_____

3) What jobs did John have in the new colony?

_____

_____

4) What did John and Elizabeth begin in 1795?

_____

5) When John was sent back to England in 1801, what did Elizabeth do?

_____

_____

6) What did John do while he was in England?

_____

7) What did John and Elizabeth Macarthur do with the help of their sons?

_____

8) What kind of person was John Macarthur?

_____

9) What did John and Elizabeth Macarthur establish in Australia?

_____

Answers: page 131

Elizabeth Farm, built at Parramatta by the Macarthurs in 1794, is Australia's oldest surviving European building,

C) Language activities – prepositions

- Prepositions are words such as: in, on, under, over, before, after, about, at, from, for, with.
- Prepositions show the relationship between nouns and other words in the sentence.

Prepositions of place include: in, on, at, between, behind, next to, near.
Read the following examples:

Write another example:

- We use 'in' to talk about enclosed places, e.g. in the car, in the room, in the cup _____

- We use 'in' to talk about limited areas, e.g. in the park, in Australia _____

- We use 'at' to talk about a particular place, e.g. at the bus stop, at home _____

- We use 'on' when we talk about surfaces, e.g. on the road, on the plate _____

- We use 'to' and 'from' to show direction of travel, e.g. **to** Australia **from** Australia

- We use 'to' and 'from' to show direction of action e.g. Give money **to** him. _____

I borrow books **from** a library. _____

Prepositions of time include: in, on, at, for, during
Read the following examples:

Write another example:

- We use 'in' to mean within a period of time, eg. in July, in 2012, in the evening _____

- We use 'at' to talk about a particular time, eg. at 2 o'clock, at lunchtime _____

- We use 'on' to talk about days and dates, e.g. on Monday, on 2nd July _____

- We use 'for' to talk about length of time, e.g. for ten years, for one hour _____

- We use 'during' to talk about known periods of time, eg, during winter _____

The **preposition 'with'** shows relationship between people and things, e.g. <u>with</u> friends, <u>with</u> money

Practice

Add prepositions to the following sentences about John and Elizabeth Macarthur.
You can use the prepositions in the box more than once.   Answers: page 131.

in	during	from	to	for	with

1) John and Elizabeth Macarthur married _____ England _____ 1788.

2) They bought Merino sheep which came _____ Spain.

3) _____ his time _____ the colony, John argued _____ the governors of the colony.

4) John was away _____ Australia _____ almost four years.

5) He showed his samples of wool _____ people _____ the British wool industry.

6) John Macarthur was allowed to return _____ the colony _____ 1817.

7) Back _____ Australia, he gave his full attention _____ developing the wool industry.

8) John and Elizabeth,_____ the help of their sons, were soon exporting wool _____ England.

Governor and Mrs Macquarie

Lachlan Macquarie was the fifth governor of Australia. During his years in the colony he and his wife, Elizabeth, made many important improvements. Later, he became known as 'The Father of Australia'.

Lachlan Macquarie was the son of a Scottish farmer. In 1810, after being a soldier for many years, he was sent to the colony of New South Wales to become the new governor. His wife, Elizabeth, went with him.

When they arrived in the colony there were many problems. The government of the colony had become weak as the military officers had become very powerful. The army officers were more interested in looking after themselves than improving the colony. They kept the convicts oppressed so they could use them as workers without paying them.

Macquarie planned to change things. He believed reformed convicts should have the same rights as free people after their time of punishment ended. He believed a policy of equality should be part of Australian society. He introduced the idea of a fair go by saying that reformed convicts should have a second chance and he encouraged them to stay in the colony rather than return to Britain.

During Macquarie's time as governor, the white population of Australia increased from 11,000 to over 38,000; this included a large increase in the number of new convicts being sent from Britain. The Macquaries had a vision for the colony. They wanted to build a place to be proud of and a place to be admired by visitors from around the world. So Governor Macquarie began a building program for government buildings, hospitals, schools, parks, churches, courthouses, lighthouses and factories. He also established a school for Aboriginal children.

They also planned new towns, roads and bridges for the colony. They organised exploration of the country beyond the coastal area of Sydney to find new land for farming and settlement. When a way was found to cross the mountains, west of Sydney, Macquarie ordered a road to be built across the mountains and established the first inland city of Bathurst.

The Macquaries made many other improvements to the colony. They organised the first official horse-race in Australia. It was part of their plan to improve the entertainment and social life of Sydney. They hoped the racecourse would be a neutral meeting place for all people; military officers, free settlers and convicts.

In 1813, Governor Macquarie introduced the first official currency of Australia. He used Spanish dollars and had the centre cut out of each one to make two new coins. These were the 'Holey Dollar' (the outer circle with a hole in the centre) and the 'Dump' (the small cut-out piece). He also established Australia's first bank, post office and postal service.

Governor and Elizabeth Macquarie advanced Australia in many ways. In remembrance of them, many places throughout Australia include their names.

A) Governor and Mrs Macquarie - Vocabulary activity

Find and highlight the following words in the story about Governor and Elizabeth Macquarie. Write them next to the appropriate meaning. The first one has been done as an example.

	equality	~~oppressed~~ ✓ reformed	policy
a fair go	a vision	admired established	social life exploration
	currency	neutral remembrance	advanced

1. _____oppressed_____ - stopped from having the same rights as other people, treated unfairly

2. _____ - improved, changed to an honest way of living and behaving

3. _____ - an idea, plan and way of acting by the government about a situation

4. _____ - a situation where people have the same rights and opportunities

5. _____ - a fair, honest and equal way of treating people

6. _____ - started a new organisation, place or activity

7. _____ - a good idea or good plan for something for the future

8. _____ - liked and thought of as very good

9. _____ - travel to unknown places to see what is there

10. _____ - when people meet together with friends to enjoy life

11. _____ - situation when people don't argue or take sides in a competition or fight

12. _____ - the system of money used by a country

13. _____ – improved, made into something better

14. _____ - as a way of remembering a person or event

Answers: page 132

Australia's first official currency:

The 'Holey Dollar'

and

The 'Dump'

Governor Macquarie introduced the first official currency of Australia. He used Spanish dollars and had the centre cut out of each one to make two new coins.

The coins were known as the 'Holey Dollar' and the 'Dump'. The outer circle with a hole in the centre was the 'Holey Dollar', while the small cut-out piece was called the 'Dump'.

B) Governor and Mrs Macquarie - Comprehension activity

Work in a group. One person should read aloud each question below.
Discuss the answer to each question together before you write anything.

1) Who was Lachlan Macquarie?

_____

2) When did he come to Australia?

_____

3) What was the situation in the NSW colony when Lachlan Macquarie arrived?

_____

4) What did Governor Macquarie believe about convicts?

_____

5) What vision did the Macquaries have for the future of the colony?

_____

6) What did their building program include?

_____

_____

7) Why did the Macquaries organise the first official horse-race?

_____

8) What did Governor Macquarie introduce in 1813?

_____

9) How did Governor Macquarie create Australia's first currency?

_____

Answers: page 132

Hyde Park Barracks was built in 1819 during Macquarie's governorship. The building still stands in Macquarie Street, Sydney.

C) Language activities - adjectives

Adjectives are words that describe someone or something. Adjectives give more information about nouns in the sentence. Adjectives often come directly before nouns.

For example:

Write another example: →

adjective	noun
fifth	governor
British	colony
new	roads
old	building

Nationality words

When talking about people or things from a particular country, we use an adjective to indicate the country. Many 'nationality' adjectives are made by changing the end of the country's name, e.g. food from Mexico is Mexican; a person from Turkey is Turkish; people from China are Chinese. Sometimes the spelling changes within the word, e.g. France - French; Denmark - Danish.

Note: Nationality adjectives always begin with a capital letter.

Practice - Complete the table with examples below. Check your answers: page 132

Country or region	Nationality adjective	Give examples by writing adjectives and nouns below:
Africa	African	e.g. the African continent
Asia		an Asian language
	Canadian	
	Chilean	
China		
Europe		
Germany		
Greece		
India		
	Italian	
Poland		
Spain		
	Swedish	
Turkey		
Vietnam		
Add more examples of countries and nationalities of people you know		

Adjectives - continued

Adjectives often come before nouns in sentences. For example:

I bought a <u>new</u> book. I met an <u>old</u> friend.

Adjectives can also be used **after** nouns with the following patterns.

Noun + verb + adjectives

Noun + verb + article + adjectives + noun.

For example: Australia is hot and dry.   **or**   Australia is a hot, dry place.

Practice with adjectives

The following sentences are about Governor and Mrs Macquarie.
Add the correct adjectives to the sentences.

fifth	important	military	Scottish	weak	powerful	reformed
free	same	coastal	Aboriginal	white	large new	social
inland	official	neutral	small	Spanish	outer	postal

Governor Macquarie

Lachlan Macquarie was the _____[1] governor of Australia. He was the son of a _____[2] farmer. During his twelve years in charge of the colony, he and Elizabeth made many _____[3] improvements. The government of the colony had become _____[4] since Governor Phillip left in 1792 because the _____[5] officers had become very _____[6].

The Macquaries believed _____[7] convicts should have the _____[8] rights as _____[9] people. They also established a school for _____[10] children. During Macquarie's time as governor, the _____[11] population of Australia increased. This included a _____[12] increase in the number of _____[13] convicts. He organised exploration of the country beyond the _____[14] area of Sydney. He ordered a road to be built across the mountains and established the first _____[15] city.

The Macquaries organised the first _____[16] horse-race in Australia as part of their plan to improve the entertainment and _____[17] life of Sydney. The racecourse was designed as a _____[18] meeting place for all people.

In 1813 Macquarie introduced the first official currency of Australia. He used _____[19] dollars and had the centre cut out of each one to make two new coins. These were the 'Holey Dollar' (the _____[20] circle with a hole in the centre) and the 'Dump' (the _____[21] cut-out piece). He also established Australia's first bank, and _____[22] service.

Answers: page 133

Adjectives - spelling practice

Using the words in the Governor Macquarie text on page 40, write the adjectives in the crossword next to the corresponding numbers.

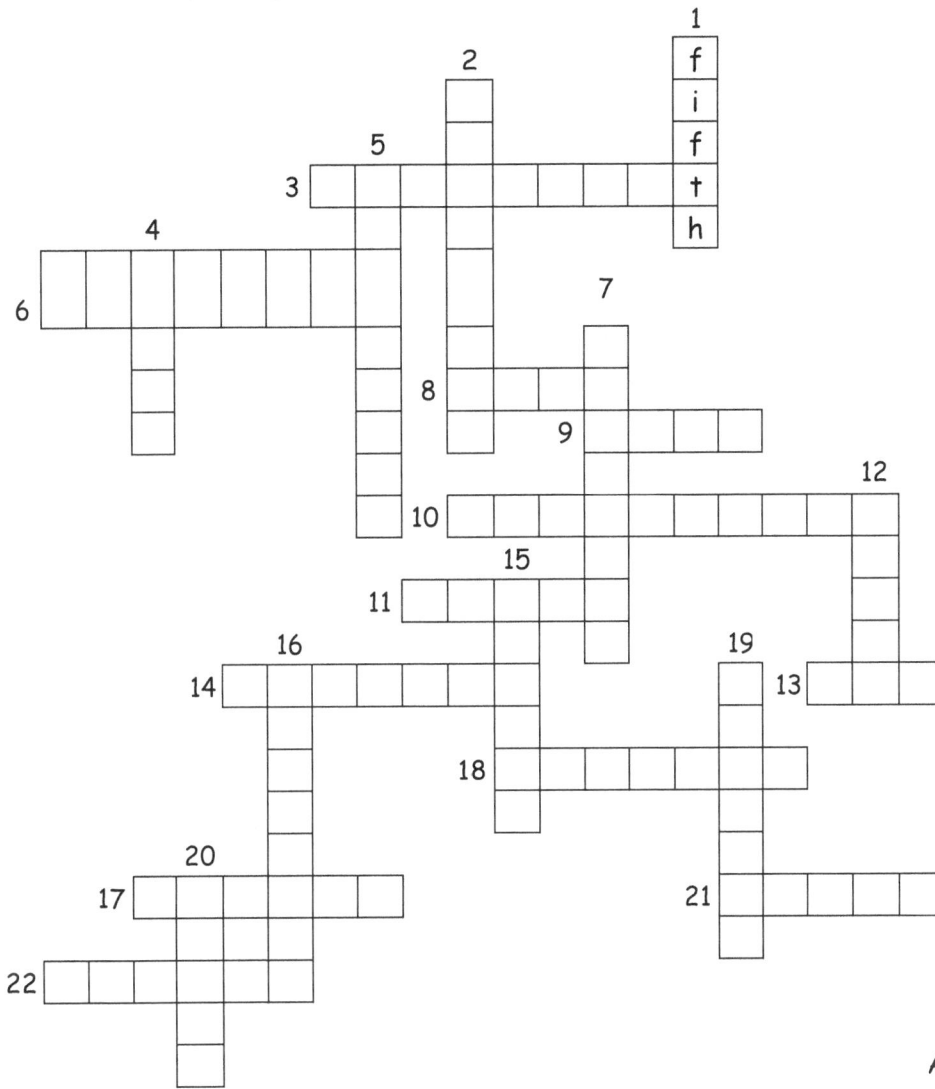

1
f
i
f
t
h

Answers: page 133

Several places in and near Australia include the name 'Macquarie'.
Use an **atlas** or **online map** to find the following places.

Macquarie Harbour   Macquarie Island   Macquarie River   Port Macquarie

Mark the approximate location
of each place on the map.

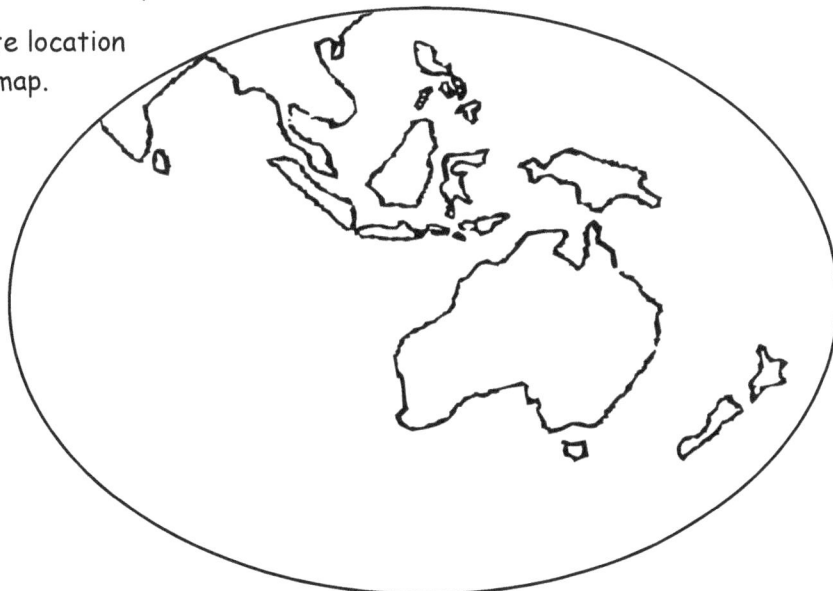

Caroline Chisholm

Caroline Chisholm was a social reformer who improved the lives of thousands of women in early Australia. She worked to reunite families and helped thousands of migrants to have a better life.

Caroline was born in England in 1808. When she was twenty-two she married Archibald Chisholm, an officer in the British Army. In 1838, they moved to Australia with their young family.

When she arrived in Sydney, Caroline was shocked to see many young homeless women sleeping on the streets. Many of these women were not convicts; they had come to Australia as free women looking for a better life. The British government encouraged young women to travel to Australia because it wanted more women in the colony. But when they arrived in Sydney there were no jobs for them in the city and there was nowhere for them to live. Caroline could not stand by and watch young women suffer in dirty, inhumane conditions. She asked Governor Gipps for the use of an old building that she could turn into a home for these desperate young women. At first the governor said no; he said it would cost too much money. But Caroline was persistent. She convinced him that her idea would help the colony as well as the young women. She worked hard to clean and prepare the old building which became a home for almost a hundred women. Caroline called it the 'Female Immigrants' Home'.

Caroline's next project was to organise an employment agency for women who needed to find jobs. She knew that many families in rural areas needed female workers to help look after their homes and children. So she started an advertising campaign to find employment for young women by sending letters to wealthy farmers.

During 1842, she met every migrant ship that arrived in Sydney, welcoming and helping the new migrants to settle into their new country. Then she personally took the young women to their new jobs in the rural areas. She went with them because many of the women were afraid to leave the city alone and were frightened of the bush. Also, she wanted to make sure they would be treated well in their new situation. Caroline Chisholm's employment agency became so successful that within a year she had found jobs and homes for almost a thousand women. She was the first person in Australia to introduce work contracts, which were agreements about working conditions and payment for workers.

Caroline's next project was to reunite the families of convicts who had been sent to Australia. She returned to England in 1846 to talk to the government about helping the husbands, wives and children of convicts to travel to Australia so that families could be together again. She travelled around Britain and Europe, even visiting the Pope, to get support for improving conditions on the ships that took convicts and free migrants to Australia. By 1853, Caroline Chisholm was one of the most famous women in England and Australia.

For thirty years Caroline continued her work of improving the lives of thousands of migrant families. All that time, she accepted no money for her work. She believed that keeping families together built a strong society and would benefit Australia. Today Caroline Chisholm is remembered as one of Australia's most outstanding women.

A) Caroline Chisholm - Vocabulary activity

Find the following words and expressions in the story about Caroline Chisholm
Write them next to the appropriate meaning. One has been done as an example.

reunite	~~social reformer~~ ✓	inhumane conditions	stand by	turn into	desperate
persistent	rural areas	convinced	advertising campaign		employment agency
	work contracts	the bush	outstanding	benefit	

1. _____social reformer_____ - a person who works to improve the living conditions of other people

2. _____ - bring together again

3. _____ - allow something bad to happen because nothing is done to stop it

4. _____ - conditions where people are in a very bad situation

5. _____ - change to a different purpose, change to become something different

6. _____ - in a bad or serious situation with little or no hope

7. _____ - continuing to do or ask something until you get what you want

8. _____ - made another person believe that something is a good idea

9. _____ - an organisation that helps people to find jobs

10. _____ - places away from the towns, in the countryside, often farming areas

11. _____ - activities to advertise that something new is going to happen

12. _____ - the wild parts of Australia, the rural areas where few people live

13. _____ _____ - agreement between employers and workers about pay and conditions

14. _____ - help to improve something

15. _____ - excellent, very special

Answers: page 134

Caroline Chisholm's picture was on Australia's $5 note from 1967 to 1992.

She was the first woman (other than Queen Elizabeth) to appear on any Australian currency.

B) Caroline Chisholm - Comprehension activity

Work in a group. One person should read aloud each question below.
Discuss the answer to each question together before you write anything.

1) Who was Caroline Chisholm?

_____

2) What was Caroline shocked to see when she arrived in Sydney?

_____

3) What did she decide to do about the living conditions of young migrant women?

_____

4) What was Caroline's next project?

_____

5) How did she organise jobs for young migrant women?

_____

6) Why did Caroline personally take the young women to their new jobs in the rural areas?

_____

7) What was she successful in doing in the first year of her employment project?

_____

8) Why did Caroline return to England in 1846?

_____

9) How much was she paid for the work she did?

_____

10) How is Caroline Chisholm remembered today?

_____

Answers: page 134

See group speaking activities on pages 116 - 120.

See a biography writing activity on page 121.

C) Language activities – personal pronouns

Pronouns are words such as *I, you, he, she, him, her, we, they, them, it.*
Pronouns are used in the place of nouns already used in previous sentences.

For example:
                                        She   she
Caroline Chisholm was a social reformer. ~~Caroline~~ was born in 1808. When ~~Caroline~~ was twenty-two
   she   they
~~Caroline~~ married Archibald Chisholm. In 1838, ~~Caroline~~ and ~~Archibald Chisholm~~ moved to Australia.

We use different pronouns to replace **subject** nouns and **object** nouns.

The subject is the person
or thing doing the action.

The object is the receiver or
one affected by the action.

subject	verb (action)	object
1. Archibald	married	Caroline.
He	married	her.
2. Mrs Chisholm	talked to	the Governor.
She	talked to	him.
3. Caroline	cleaned	the old building.
She	cleaned	it.
4. Caroline	helped	the young migrant women.
She	helped	them.
5. The young women	thanked	Caroline.
They	thanked	her.

subject pronouns		object pronouns	
the person or thing doing the action		person or thing affected by the action	
single	**plural**	**single**	**plural**
I	we	me	us
you	you	you	you
he/she/it	they	him/her/it	them

Practice - Complete the following text with the correct pronoun from the box.

she	he	they	it	them	him

                      (Caroline)
When Caroline arrived in Sydney, _____ saw many young homeless women sleeping on the streets.
                              (the women)
Many of these women were not convicts; _____ had come to Australia looking for a better life.
       (the women)   (the women)
But when _____ arrived in Sydney there were no jobs for _____ and there was nowhere for
(the women)   (the women)
_____ to live. Caroline asked Governor Gipps for the use of an old building for _____.
                        (the governor)   (the old building)
At first the governor said no; _____ said _____ would cost too much money. But Caroline was
               (the governor)   (Caroline)
persistent. She convinced _____ that her idea would help the colony. _____ worked hard to
                                                (the old building)
clean and prepare the old building which became a home for almost a hundred women. She called _____
the 'Female Immigrants' Home'.

Adding the suffix 'ment' to a verb to make a noun

Some English verbs can be made into nouns by adding the suffix 'ment'.

A suffix is a group of letters added to the **end** of a word to change its meaning or function.

<u>Underline</u> examples of nouns with the suffix 'ment' in the text about Caroline Chisholm below:

> Caroline Chisholm started an advertising campaign to find employment for young migrant women by sending letters to wealthy farmers. She was the first person in Australia to introduce work contracts which were agreements about working conditions and payment for workers.

Look at the examples below which show the way we can form nouns from verbs.

verb	verb meaning	suffix to form a noun	noun name of a process or experience
employ agree pay	to pay someone to do work to have the same opinion to give money for something	add 'ment' to the verb	employment agreement payment

Look at some more examples of ways to use the suffix 'ment' to form nouns.

Complete this column:

verb	verb meaning	suffix to form a noun	noun name of a process or experience
1. retire 2. assess 3. move 4. state 5. equip 6. manage 7. settle 8. improve 9. disagree 10. punish 11. amuse 12. enjoy	to stop working to check, test or judge something to go to a different place to say or write something to include the things needed to look after or control something to go to a new place and live there to make better to have a different opinion to make someone suffer to make someone laugh to get pleasure from something	add 'ment' to the verb	1. retirement 2. 3. 4. 5. 6. 7. 8. 9. 10. 11. 12.

Write **nouns** with the suffix 'ment' in the crossword, next to its corresponding number.

Answers: p. 134

Note: The examples above provide a sample list of some words with the suffix 'ment'.

Social services - research and presentation

Today there are many organisations that help communities or individual people in various ways. Usually these organisations are operated with volunteer workers.

Your task is to find out more information about one community service organisation.

Step 1)
Choose a social service or community service organisation that you'd like to know more about.

Here are a few suggestions:

The Smith Family	Oxfam Australia
Rotary Clubs	Mission Australia
Lions (Clubs) Australia	Volunteering Australia
Starlight Children's Foundation	APEX Australia
Volunteer Fire Brigades	UNICEF
Surf Life Saving Australia	WIRES

Step 2)
Find information about the organisation or service, using one or more of the following ways:

a) look in your local newspaper, library
or
b) search the internet

Step 3)
Collect information about the organisation or service.

Step 4)
Summarise 'key information' about the organisation, answering questions such as:

- What is the name of the organisation?

- Who does the organisation aim to help?

- What kind of help do they give?

- Do they need volunteers?

- Where can we get more information?

Step 5)
Tell your classmates about the service or organisation in a short presentation.

Don't just read the information aloud - put the information into your own words.

Edmund Barton

Edmund Barton was the first Prime Minister of Australia. He was one of the people who started Australia's transition from being six separate British colonies to becoming a whole nation.

Before Edmund Barton became Prime Minister, there were six separate colonies in different places around the continent of Australia. Barton strongly believed in the idea of a Federation of Australia. This meant that Australia's six colonies should join together to be one nation. Barton worked very hard to develop a Constitution for the Federation of Australia which eventually happened in 1901. After that, Australia became known as the Commonwealth of Australia.

Edmund Barton was born in Sydney, New South Wales in 1849. He was a very good student at school and at university. After university, he worked as a lawyer in Sydney and in 1879 he became a member of the government of the New South Wales colony.

Between the years of 1880 and 1900 there was a lot of discussion about the future of Australia. At that time, the six colonies around the country had their own laws and each colony had different ideas about the way things should happen. The colonies were called New South Wales, Queensland, South Australia, Tasmania, Victoria and Western Australia. People around the country started to talk about the idea of coming together, as one nation, instead of being six small colonies; but not everyone agreed.

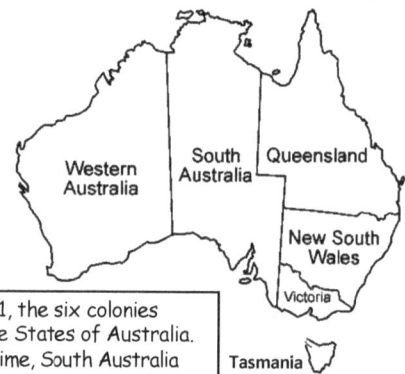

In 1901, the six colonies became the States of Australia. At that time, South Australia governed the Northern Territory.

Barton made many speeches to get people to agree about the idea of a federation. One of the famous things he said was:

'For the first time in the world's history, there will be a nation for a continent, and a continent for a nation.' Barton worked unpaid for many years with a small group of men to develop a Constitution that would be the basis for the laws of Australia. Many changes were made to the words of the Constitution before the British government gave their agreement. Also, just before Federation, the people of the Australian colonies were invited to vote to agree on the Constitution. This was the beginning of Australia's democracy.

When the Australian colonies joined together, Barton was asked to act as Prime Minister until an election was held. He was then elected as the first Prime Minister of the Commonwealth of Australia. At the time of Federation in 1901, the High Court of Australia was also formed. The High Court is the most powerful court in Australia and its role is to make sure the laws of Australia's Constitution are followed correctly. When Barton left the position of Prime Minister in 1903, he became a judge of the High Court of Australia.

Edmund Barton is remembered as a person who worked hard for something he believed strongly about and for his contribution to Australia's democracy.

A) Edmund Barton - Vocabulary activity

Find and highlight the following words and expressions in the story about Edmund Barton. Write them next to their appropriate meaning. The first one has been done as an example.

separate	colonies	transition ✓	nation	continent	Constitution
	Federation	democracy	election	Commonwealth	speeches
	lawyer	role	court	judge	contribution

1. _____transition_____ - when there is a change from one way of doing something to another way

2. _____ - not joined together, not related to each other

3. _____ - countries, or parts of countries ruled by a more powerful country

4. _____ - the people of one country

5. _____ - one of the large areas of land on the earth, such as Asia, Africa, Australia

6. _____ - a group of countries or groups of people joined together as a nation

7. _____ - a set of written laws that a government must follow

8. _____ - a democratic country that was under British rule in the past

9. _____ - a person who gives advice about the law and works in a law court

10. _____ - formal talks given to groups of people

11. _____ - system of government where people decide and vote for their leader

12. _____ – a time when people choose or vote for a leader

13. _____ – a place where decisions about laws and punishment happen

14. _____ – the job that something or someone does

15. _____ – the person in court who decides the punishment of a person

16. _____ – something that someone does to help other people or to make something successful

Answers: page 135

B) Edmund Barton - Comprehension activity

Re-read the story about Edmund Barton and answer the questions below.
Working with a partner, discuss each question before writing your answer. Answers: page 135

1) Why is Edmond Barton famous?

_____

2) Where and when was Edmund Barton born?

_____

3) What was Australia like before Edmund Barton was Prime Minister?

_____

4) What important writing did he help to develop?

_____

5) When did the Federation of Australia happen?

_____

6) The names of the colonies of Australia are now the names of the six states.
   What are the names of the six states of Australia?

_____   _____   _____

_____   _____   _____

7) What is the Constitution?

_____

8) Who were invited to agree on the Constitution before Federation happened?

_____

9) What did Edmond Barton do in 1903?

_____

10) What is the role of the High Court of Australia?

_____

Write the states and territories
on the map of modern Australia:

WA = Western Australia
NT = Northern Territory
QLD = Queensland
NSW = New South Wales
VIC = Victoria
SA = South Australia
ACT = Australian Capital Territory
TAS = Tasmania

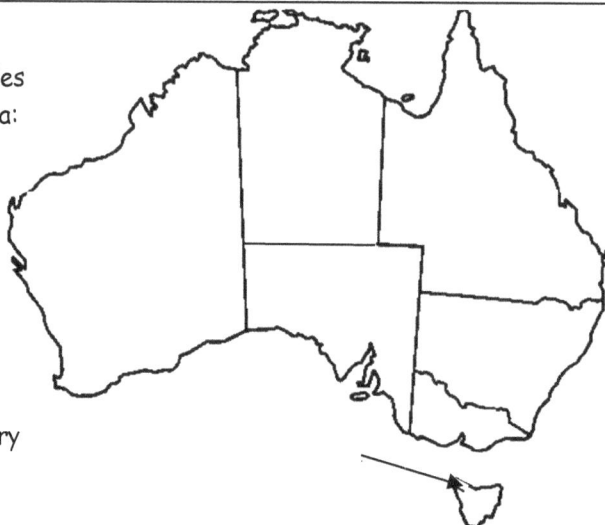

C) Language activities – punctuation: capital letters

Capital letters give readers useful information.

They are used to begin a new sentence, showing when a new idea begins.
They are used to show the names and titles of people. (eg. <u>D</u>octor <u>S</u>mith, <u>M</u>iss <u>J</u>ones)
They are used to show the names of countries, nationalities, states, cities and languages.
They are used to show the names of days and months and special events. (eg. <u>M</u>other's <u>D</u>ay)
They are used to show the titles of organizations, books or important pieces of writing.

Find examples from the story about Barton and put them in the correct place in the table below.

Titles and names of people	Names of countries
Names of nationalities	Name or title of an organisation
Names of states	Name of a city
Name of a special event	Title of a book or important writing

Capital letters – practice

Use a red pen to correct the text below by putting capital letters in the correct places.

edmund barton was born in sydney, new south wales in 1849. he was a very good student at school and at university. after university, he worked as a lawyer in sydney and in 1879 he became a member of the government of the new south wales colony.

between the years of 1880 and 1900 there was a lot of discussion about the future of australia. at that time, the six colonies around the country had their own laws and each colony had different ideas about the way things should happen. the colonies were called new south wales, queensland, south australia, tasmania, victoria and western australia. people around the country started to talk about the idea of coming together as one nation instead of being six small colonies; but not everyone agreed.

when the australian colonies joined together, barton was asked to act as prime minister until an election was held. he was then elected as the first prime minister of the commonwealth of australia. at the time of federation in 1901, the high court of australia was also formed. the high court is the most powerful court in australia and its role is to make sure the laws of australia's constitution are followed correctly. when barton left the position of prime minister in 1903, he became a judge of the high court of australia.

Check your work against the Edmund Barton text on page 48 (paragraphs 3, 4 and 6).
You should have added 54 capital letters to the above text. Answers: page 135 - 136.

Using the suffix 'ion' to form nouns

As well as being names of people and things, nouns can be the names of experiences and conditions. These nouns are **abstract nouns**; they are names for things we can **experience** but can't see or touch. Examples of abstract nouns are words such as 'idea', 'discussion' and 'communication'.

In English, abstract nouns can be formed from some verbs by adding the suffix 'ion'. Look at the following examples from the Edmund Barton text:

verb	verb meaning	suffix and spelling changes to form a noun	noun: name of experience, event or condition
discuss	to talk	add 'ion' to the verb	discussion
elect	to choose by vote	add 'ion' to the verb	election
constitute	to form or compose	take off final 'e', add 'tion'	constitution
contribute	to give	take off final 'e', add 'tion'	contribution
federate	to join	take off final 'e', add 'tion'	federation

Look at some more examples of ways to use the suffix 'ion' to form nouns

Complete this column:

verb	verb meaning	suffix and spelling changes to form a noun	noun: name of experience, event or condition
suggest	to tell or give an idea	add 'ion' to the verb	suggestion
act	to do	add 'ion'	action
construct	to build	add 'ion'	
collect	to bring together	add 'ion'	
connect	to join things	add 'ion'	
possess	to own	add 'ion'	
progress	to improve	add 'ion'	
express	to say or show	add 'ion'	
depress	to make low	add 'ion'	
pollute	to make dirty	take off final 'e', add 'ion'	
populate	to live in	take off final 'e', add 'ion'	
operate	to use equipment	take off final 'e', add 'ion'	
illustrate	to show by pictures	take off final 'e', add 'ion'	
communicate	to express ideas	take off final 'e', add 'ion'	
revise	to see/study again	take off final 'e', add 'ion'	
invite	to ask someone to come	take off final 'e', add 'ation'	
examine	to look, check or test	take off final 'e', add 'ation'	
transport	to take to another place	add 'ation'	
form	to make	add 'ation'	
inform	to tell	add 'ation'	

Note: The above examples are not a complete list of spelling variations for words with the suffix 'ion'. To find the noun form of a verb, always check your dictionary; the verb and noun forms are generally listed consecutively.

Words with suffix 'ion' – spelling practice

Make nouns from the following verbs by changing the spelling appropriately and adding the suffix 'ion'.
Write the words in the crossword next to the numbers.

1. act ✓

2. construct ✓

3. constitute

4. communicate

5. populate

6. inform

7. progress

8. express

9. collect

10. federate

11. possess

12. elect

13. suggest

14. educate

15. discuss

16. depress

17. invite

18. illustrate

19. revise

20. operate

21. transport

22. examine

23. connect

24. pollute

Answers: page 136

Edith Cowan

Edith Cowan was the first woman to be elected to an Australian parliament. She promoted migrant welfare, as well as children's and women's rights.

Edith was born in Geraldton, in Western Australia in 1861.

She did not have an easy childhood. When she was seven years old her mother died in childbirth, and her father sent her away to a boarding school in Perth. Her father remarried, but the marriage was unhappy and he began to drink too much alcohol. When Edith was only fifteen, he killed his second wife and was hanged for the crime. These experiences made Edith a serious young woman who thought a lot about the difficult situations faced by people; especially women and children.

At the age of seventeen she married James Cowan, who became a police officer in the Perth court. Over the next twelve years they had four daughters and a son. During that time she became concerned with social issues and the unjust way she believed some people were treated by the legal system. She was particularly concerned about women's health and the welfare of disadvantaged groups, such as young children, unmarried mothers and migrant groups. She wanted to make life better for these people through migrant welfare, baby health centres and equal rights for women so she joined many different organisations to help disadvantaged people. In 1909 she helped to start the Women's Service Guild which promoted equal rights for men and women. She believed better education was needed to bring change to people's lives and worked hard to improve government schools. During World War One, she collected food and clothing for soldiers and helped to care for soldiers when they returned from war.

In 1920, for the first time in Australia, women were allowed to compete for a position in parliament. In 1921 Edith became the first woman to be elected to an Australian parliament. Also, in that year she was awarded the 'Order of the British Empire' for her charity work with the Red Cross.

A clock tower was built in Perth in 1934 in memory of Edith's many good works and her life of service.

Edith Cowan has been described as 'one of Australia's greatest women'. You can see her picture on Australia's fifty dollar note. The 'Edith Cowan University' in Perth, Western Australia is named after her.

A) Edith Cowan - vocabulary activity

Find and highlight the following words and expressions in the story about Edith Cowan.
Write them next to their appropriate meaning. The first one has been done as an example.

promoted	~~elected~~ ✓	rights	welfare	boarding school	hanged
court	serious	concerned	unjust	social issues	legal system
	disadvantaged groups		awarded	parliament	

1. _____elected_____ - chosen by the people for a job in the government

2. _____ - helped something to develop; tried to make something happen

3. _____ - health, happiness, safety and well-being

4. _____ - things that people are allowed to do and have

5. _____ - a school where students live away from their family

6. _____ - killed by hanging with a rope put around the neck

7. _____ - describing a person who is quiet, not laughing very much

8. _____ - a place where decisions about laws and punishment happen

9. _____ - worried

10. _____ - issues about the way people live, such as health and housing

11. _____ - unfair, not a good or right way of treatment

12. _____ - the way of the laws in the country

13. _____ - groups of people who don't have the same chances and help as most people in society

14. _____ - the people who are part of the government where laws of the country are made

15. _____ - given a special prize for doing something good

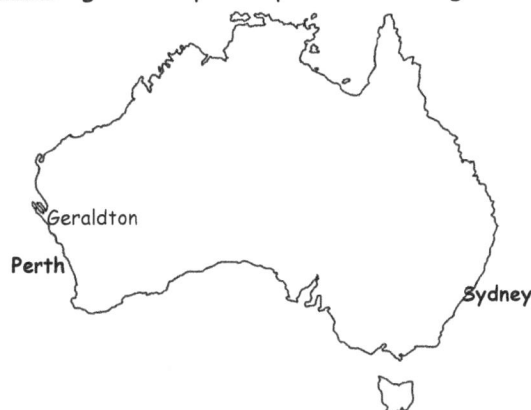

Answers: page 137

Geraldton

Perth

Sydney

B) Edith Cowan - comprehension activity

Work in a group. One person should read aloud each question below.
Discuss the answer to each question together before you write anything. Answers, page 137.

1) Why is Edith Cowan famous?

_____

2) Where and when was she born?

_____

3) Why was her childhood not easy?

_____

_____

4) What issues was she concerned about?

_____

_____

5) What did she want to do?

_____

6) What happened for the first time in Australia in 1920?

_____

7) What happened in 1921?

_____

8) Which Australian banknote shows a picture of Edith Cowan?

Australia's bank notes

Australia's banknotes are made of polymer (a type of plastic).
They have special security features to protect against illegal copying.
Each of Australia's banknotes has a picture of a significant person, as
well as other interesting images and features .

Online research:

Go to www.banknotes.rba.gov.au/banknote-features/ to see all the people and features on Australia's banknotes.

What am I? Choose an image or feature on a banknote and describe it to your group.
They must guess what it is and say which banknote displays the image or feature.

Design a banknote:

Imagine it is your job to design a new Australian banknote.
Decide who will feature on your banknote and research their achievements.
Design images to show what they have done.
Present your design and explain its features.

For more activities on Australia's banknotes, go to https://banknotes.rba.gov.au/games/

Australian Banknotes

$5 note: Front: Her Majesty Queen Elizabeth II   Back: Australia's Parliament House

$5

Whose picture can you see on the **$10 note**?

Front: _____   Back: _____

$10

Whose picture can you see on the **$20 note**?

Front: _____   Back: _____

$20

Whose picture can you see on the **$50 note**?

Front: _____   Back: _____

$50

Whose picture can you see on the **$100 note**?

Front: _____   Back: _____

$100

Answers: page 137

What other images and features you can see on each banknote?

Go to: www.banknotes.rba.gov.au/banknote-features/ for more information.

'Banjo' Paterson

Banjo Paterson was a famous Australian writer. He wrote stories and poems about the Australian bush and about the people who lived and worked there. He wrote 'Waltzing Matilda' which became one of Australia's best known songs.

Banjo Paterson's real name was Andrew Barton Paterson.
'Banjo' was a nickname he used when he first started writing and he has been known as 'Banjo' Paterson ever since then.

He was born in a small country town near Orange, in New South Wales, in 1864. When he was a young boy, his family moved to a farm near Yass where he enjoyed his childhood and learnt to love horses and the Australian bush.

Yass is a country town close to the main highway between Sydney and Melbourne. While he lived there, 'Banjo' saw people travelling in coaches, horse riders from the Snowy Mountains and drovers on horses taking sheep and cattle across the country. These were the people and places he wrote about later in his stories and poems.

In 1874, when he was ten years old, he was sent to school in Sydney where he lived with his grandmother. After he finished school he worked in a lawyer's office and after a few years, he became a lawyer. Although he worked in the city, his stories and poems show his love of the bush.

In 1895, he wrote the ballads 'The Man from Snowy River' and 'Waltzing Matilda' which were published in the newspaper. His stories quickly became very popular and were soon published in books. Seven thousand copies sold in a few months and more books were quickly re-printed. 'Banjo' soon became famous in Australia and overseas. Now 'Waltzing Matilda' has become Australia's most famous song.

As well as being a writer of Australian stories, Banjo Paterson worked as a journalist in Africa and China. During World War One, he was a soldier and later drove an ambulance. He also made three voyages with horses to Africa, China and Egypt, as a volunteer vet.

He was a great Australian, who wrote funny stories about characters in the Australian outback and beautiful poems about the hardships and the pleasures of living in the Australian bush. His picture is on Australia's ten dollar note.

A) Banjo Paterson - Vocabulary activity

Find and highlight the following words and expressions in the story about Banjo Paterson. Write them next to their appropriate meaning. One has been done as an example.

nickname	~~poems~~ ✓	the Australian bush	coaches	lawyer	drovers
ballads	popular	published	volunteer	voyages	vet
	characters	hardships	outback	pleasures	

1. _____*poems*_____ - pieces of writing that have words that rhyme, have the same sound

2. _____ - an informal name, often used by friends instead of a real name

3. _____ - the wild parts of Australia, away from the towns and cities

4. _____ - transport pulled by horses, used to take people from one place to another place

5. _____ - people who move sheep or cattle across the country

6. _____ - a person who gives advice about the law and works in a law court

7. _____ - songs that tell a story

8. _____ - printed in a book, newspaper or magazine

9. _____ - liked by many people

10. _____ - long trips to another place by ship

11. _____ - a person who works without payment of money

12. _____ - a person who gives medical help to sick animals

13. _____ – interesting people

14. _____ – the wild, open inland parts of Australia, away from the cities

15. _____ – problems or difficult situations

16. _____ – happiness and enjoyment

Answers: page 138

B) Banjo Paterson - Comprehension activity

Re-read the story about Banjo Paterson and answer the questions.
Discuss the answers with a partner before writing them below.

1) Why is Banjo Paterson famous?

_____

2) Is 'Banjo' his real name?

_____

3) Where did he live when he was a child?

_____

4) What did he see when he was a boy living near Yass?

_____

5) What job did he have after he left school?

_____

6) When did he write the ballad, 'Walzing Matilda'?_____

7) What were his stories and poems about?

_____

8) Which Australian money shows a picture of 'Banjo' Paterson?

_____   Answers: page 138

Plural nouns - 'Plural' means 'more than one thing'.

There are spelling and pronunciation rules to follow when we change nouns to their plural forms,

- With most nouns, we add 's' to make the plural form.
  Write plural nouns from the story about Banjo Paterson on the lines below.

noun	plural noun	noun	plural noun
poem	*poems*_____	place	_____
horse	_____	drover	_____
rider	_____	year	_____
book	_____	character	_____

- When nouns end with 's' , 'sh' or 'ch', we add 'es'. For example: a watch → watches
                                                                    a beach → beaches

	noun	plural noun	noun	plural noun
Check the following words in a dictionary	coach	_____	class	_____
Write the spelling of their plural nouns:	bus	_____	wish	_____

C) Language activities - spelling and pronunciation of plural nouns

When nouns end with y, we change y to 'ies' to make plurals. Write plural nouns below from Banjo's story:	Sometimes we use a different word to mean 'plural'. For example: one mouse – six mice Write plural nouns below from Banjo's story:
singular noun **plural noun**	**singular noun** **plural noun**
story _____	person _____
copy _____	cow _____
	Note: A few nouns have <u>the same spelling</u> to mean singular or plural, e.g. one <u>sheep</u> - six <u>sheep</u>

Spelling practice – plural nouns

Change the nouns below to their plural form. Write the plural form in the crossword next to the corresponding numbers. One has been done as an example.

1. place = *places*✓
2. page
3. family
4. horse
5. character
6. beach
7. copy
8. city
9. song
10. class
11. person
12. country
13. sheep
14. story
15. year
16. glass

Answers: page 138

Pronunciation of words ending with 'es'

'es' endings on words are sometimes pronounced as an extra syllable.
The pronunciation of 'es' depends on the sound it follows. Look at the examples below.

'es' is pronounced as an extra syllable after *s, sh, ch, c, g*		After most letters, 'es' is not an extra syllable. All the example words below have one syllable
one syllable	adding *es* or *s* makes two syllables	
horse	hor<u>s</u>es	note notes (adding 'es' does **not** add an
coach	coa<u>ch</u>es	name names extra syllable to these words)
place	pla<u>c</u>es	date dates
glass	glas<u>s</u>es	side sides
stage	sta<u>g</u>es	line lines

Banjo Paterson's ballad 'Waltzing Matilda'

People have different ideas about the meaning of 'Waltzing Matilda' because the ballad was written with words that people don't use now.

Just as Paterson's nickname was 'Banjo', other things were given nicknames. For example, the word 'waltzing' meant 'walking from place to place'.

In the late 1800's some men travelled around the country looking for work. Also, the backpack, or the bag he carried on his back with all his personal possessions and bedroll, was called his 'Matilda'.
So, 'Waltzing Matilda' meant 'walking around the country with a backpack on your back'.

Below is a version of the song that most people know today.

Photo: Swagman holding a billy and carrying a swag on his back.

Waltzing Matilda

Once a jolly swagman camped by a billabong
Under the shade of a coolibah tree
And he sang as he watched and waited till his billy boiled
You'll come a waltzing Matilda with me.

Waltzing Matilda, Waltzing Matilda
You'll come a-waltzing Matilda with me
And he sang as he watched and waited till his billy boiled
You'll come a-waltzing Matilda with me.

Down came a jumbuck to drink at that billabong
Up jumped the swagman and grabbed him with glee
And he sang as he shoved that jumbuck in his tuckerbag
You'll come a-waltzing Matilda with me.

Waltzing Matilda, Waltzing Matilda
You'll come a-waltzing Matilda with me
And he sang as he watched and waited till his billy boiled
You'll come a-waltzing Matilda with me.

Up rode the squatter mounted on his thoroughbred
Down came troopers one two three
Whose that jumbuck you've got in the tuckerbag?
You'll come a-waltzing Matilda with me.

Waltzing Matilda, Waltzing Matilda
You'll come a-waltzing Matilda with me
And he sang as he watched and waited till his billy boiled
You'll come a-waltzing Matilda with me.

Up jumped the swagman and sprang into the billabong
You'll never catch me alive said he.
And his ghost may be heard as you pass by that billabong
You'll come a-waltzing Matilda with me.

(This version of Banjo Paterson's ballad was produced by Marie Cowan in 1903)

Paraphrasing Banjo Paterson's ballad 'Waltzing Matilda'

'Paraphrasing' means writing or saying something in a different or simpler way, using words that make the meaning clearer or easier to understand.

Find and highlight the words from **Waltzing Matilda** ballad on page 62.

Words from
Waltzing Matilda   **meaning**

jolly	=	happy
swagman		man who travels the countryside with his pack of belongings on his back
billabong		waterhole
coolibah tree		tree (a type of Australian eucalyptus tree)
billy		a metal cooking pot for boiling water and heating food
waltzing		walking around the countryside (looking for work on farms etc)
matilda		a backpack (containing all personal possessions)
a jumbuck		a sheep
tuckerbag		food bag or sack for carrying food
the squatter		the farmer (who owned the sheep)
thoroughbred		expensive horse
troopers		policemen
ghost		spirit of a dead person

Paraphrasing practice

Complete the paraphrased version of the story of Waltzing Matilda below, using words from the list above to make the <u>meaning</u> clearer. The first one has been done as an example.

jolly swagman
The ballad of Waltzing Matilda tells the story of a <u>happy traveller</u> who travels the countryside looking for work in outback Australia.

swagman   billabong
The story explains that the _____ camped by a _____, under the shade

coolibah tree   billy
of a _____. As he waited till water in his _____ boiled, he sang,

jumbuck
'You'll come a-waltzing Matilda with me'. As he sat by his campfire, along came a _____ to drink

billabong   jumbuck   tuckebag
at the _____. He grabbed the _____ and put it in his _____ for later.

squatter   thoroughbred
Just then, along came the _____ on his _____ and three

troopers   jumbuck   tuckerbag
_____ on horses. They asked him, 'Whose is that _____ you've got in the _____?

troopers   billabong
The swagman didn't want the _____ to catch him so he jumped into the _____
where he drowned. The story tells that if you pass by that billabong now, the swagman's ghost
can be heard singing, 'You'll come a-waltzing Matilda with me.'

People in Australia's Past   63   www.boyereducation.com.au

Nellie Melba

Nellie Melba was an Australian woman who became a world famous classical singer. Her picture can be seen on Australia's hundred dollar note.

Nellie was born in Melbourne in 1861. As a young woman, she moved to Queensland where she met and married Charles Armstrong.

Nellie had studied music and singing at school and wanted to become a professional singer but her husband didn't like the idea and did everything he could to stop her. However, Nellie was determined to follow her dream and in 1884 she left Queensland to begin a singing career in Melbourne. With the help of other musicians, she organised performances at the Melbourne Town Hall. At the same time, she began planning a trip to Europe to audition for roles in operas.

At first she did not find the success she wanted in London, so she went to Paris. In Paris she was taught by a famous singing teacher who advised her to choose a stage name, so she decided to use the name 'Melba' as a contraction of her hometown of Melbourne. In 1887, Nellie gave her first successful European performance in Brussels. From that time, she became well known as 'Nellie Melba', singing with great success in London, Paris, Milan, New York and other major cities.

'Melba' soon became world-famous. She was invited to sing before Queen Victoria of England and gave performances for presidents, kings and queens in Europe. When she appeared in European cities she was greeted by crowds of people, as movie stars are today. In 1902, she returned to Australia as a superstar. She travelled throughout Australia and New Zealand, giving concerts in the capital cities. In that year she set a new world record by earning more for a single performance than any other musical artist in the world. In 1920 she became the first international musician to do radio broadcasts.

During the First World War, she worked tirelessly to raise money for charities which helped people suffering in the war. After the war, she was made a 'Dame of the British Empire', which was a special title she received for her charity work. It was the first time the award had been given to an entertainer. In 1927, on the day Canberra became Australia's capital city she sang the national anthem at the official opening of Australia's Parliament House.

In 1928, she gave her final concerts in Australia and left for Europe to sing farewell concerts in London, Paris and Egypt. She was in her sixties by then but still attracted very large audiences. When Melba died in Sydney in 1931, her funeral was a national event. Her funeral procession was almost two kilometres long.

Nellie Melba was loved by millions of people around the world. She was a great achiever and she was Australia's first superstar.

Crowds lined the streets for Nellie Melba's funeral in 1931.

A) Nellie Melba - Vocabulary activity

Find the following words and expressions in the story about Nellie Melba and write them next to the appropriate meaning. The first one has been done as an example.

classical   stage name   performances   determined   audition   operas

contraction   radio broadcasts   achiever

tirelessly   farewell   audiences   charities   funeral procession

1. _____classical_____ - relating to music that is considered traditional rather than modern

2. _____ - wanting to do something very much and not letting anything stop you

3. _____ - events of singing, acting and music to entertain people

4. _____ - when singers do a short performance to show their ability to get a job

5. _____ - musical performances where the words of a story are sung

6. _____ - name used by an entertainer that is different to their real name

7. _____ - a word that is made shorter

8. _____ - programs sent out by radio for people to listen to

9. _____ - working very hard, without stopping to rest

10. _____ - organisations that give help and money to people in difficult situations

11. _____ - goodbye

12. _____ - groups of people watching or listening to a performance

13. _____ - special ceremony when someone dies and people move slowly in a line

14. _____ - someone who is successful by working hard to reach their goal

Answers: page 139

B) Nellie Melba - Comprehension activity

Work in a group. One person should read aloud each question below.
Discuss the answer to each question together before you write anything.

1) Who was Nellie Melba?

_____

2) Where and when was she born?

_____

3) Why did Nellie return to Melbourne from Queensland?

_____

4) Why did she choose the name 'Melba' for herself ?

_____

5) Who did Nellie give performances for?

_____

6) What 'world record' did Nellie Melba make?

_____

7) Why was Nellie Melba made a Dame of the British Empire?

_____

8) What was the special event when she sang in Canberra?

_____

9) How old was Nellie Melba when she gave her final concerts?

_____

10) Where can we see a picture of Nellie Melba?

_____

Answers: page 139

See group speaking activities on pages 116 - 120.

See a biography writing activity on page 121.

C) Language activities - phrases that show time or place

A phrase is a group of two or more words that go together to show meaning within a sentence.
A phrase doesn't include a verb so it isn't the same as a sentence.

Phrases of **time** tell **when** something happened.
Phrases of **place** tell **where** something happened.

Look at the following examples from the story about Nellie Melba.

phrase of place · phrase of time · phrase of time · phrase of place
Nellie was born **in Melbourne** **in 1861**. **As a young girl**, she moved **to Queensland**.
phrase of time · phrase of place
In 1884 she left Queensland to begin a singing career **in Melbourne**. She organized
phrase of place · phrase of time
performances **at the Melbourne Town Hall**. **At the same time**, she began planning a trip
phrase of place · phrase of place
to Europe to audition for roles **in operas**.

Phrases of time or place that begin with a preposition are called prepositional phrases.

Look at the examples:

Phrases of time	Phrases of place
in 1861	in Melbourne
as a young woman	to Queensland
in 1884	at the Melbourne Town Hall
at the same time	to Europe
	in operas

Read the story of Nellie Melba and highlight the phrases that show **time**.
Read the story of Nellie Melba and highlight the phrases that show **place**,
using a different colour.

Add more examples from the story to the table above.
Answers, page 140

On the right, you can see a statue of Dame Nellie Melba
by sculptor, Peter Corlett at Waterfront City in Melbourne.

Using the suffix 'al' to form adjectives

Some English nouns can be made into adjectives by adding the suffix 'al'.
Adjectives ending in 'al' usually have the meaning 'relating to something'.
For example, the adjective 'musical' means 'relating to music'.

<u>Underline</u> examples of adjectives with the suffix 'al ' in the text about Nellie Melba below:

Nellie Melba was a world famous classical singer. In 1902, she set a new world record by earning more for a single performance than any other musical artist in the world. In 1920 she became the first international musician to do radio broadcasts.

Look at the following examples from the Nellie Melba text which show the way we can form adjectives from some nouns:

noun	meaning	suffix to form an adjective	adjective - relating to or having the quality of something
a classic	a book or film or music that has been popular for a long time	add 'al'	classical
a profession	a job that needs special training or education		professional
a nation	the people living in a country		national

Spelling tip: For words ending with a silent letter 'e' , remove the 'e' before adding 'al' to make an adjective. e.g. globe → global

Complete this column

noun	meaning	suffix and spelling change to form an adjective	adjective – relating to or having the quality of something
1. coast	land beside the ocean	add 'al' to the noun	1. coastal
2. music	sounds or singing ♪ ♫		2.
3. post	mail (letters)		3.
4. origin	beginning		4.
5. herb	a plant used in cooking		5.
6. region	area		6.
7. profession	job of special training		7.
8. digit	number		8.
9. centre	middle	remove the silent 'e' then add 'al'	9.
10. medicine	something to fix illness		10.
11. culture	traditions of a country		11.
12. globe	world		12.
13. tide	rise and fall of the sea		13.
14. tribe	a group of people		14.

Adjectives crossword

Write **adjectives** from page 68 next to the corresponding numbers in the crossword.

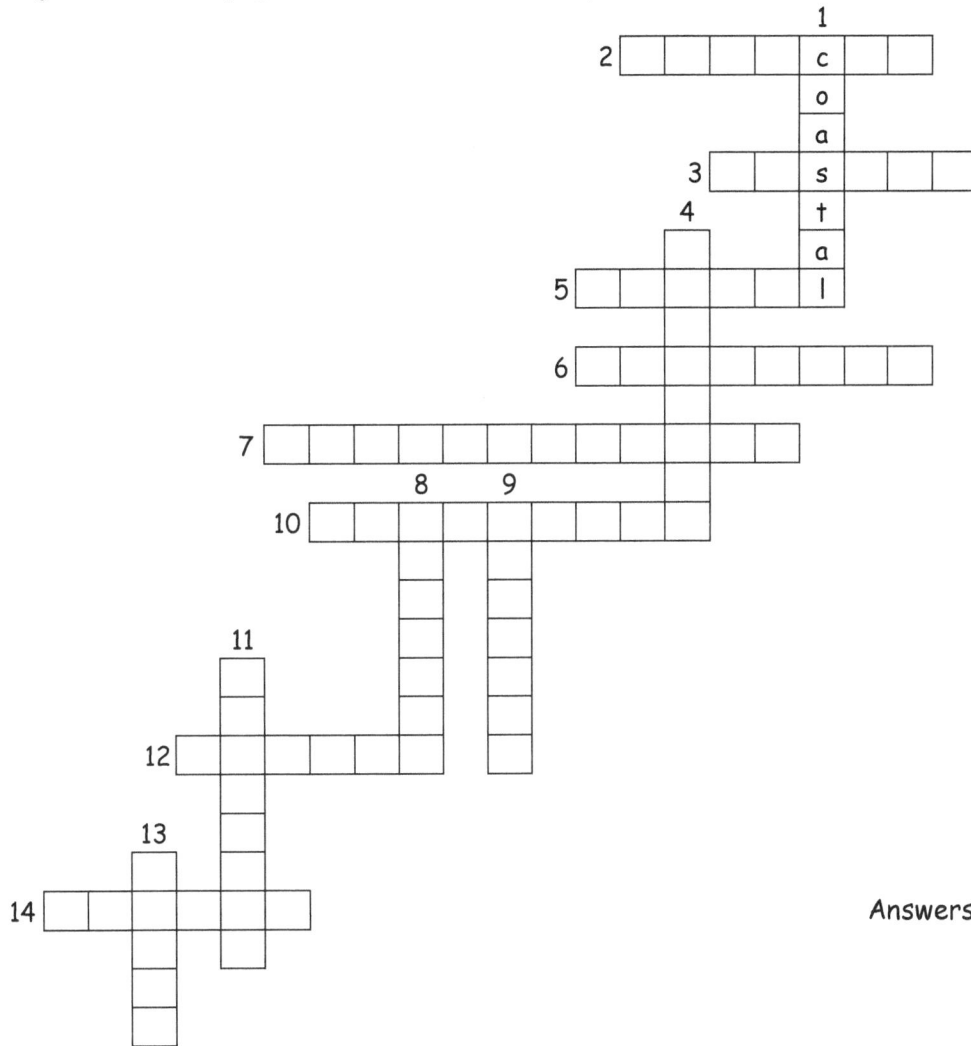

```
                                          1
                          2 □ □ □ □ c □ □
                                    o
                                    a
                          3 □ □ □ s □ □ □
                     4 □
                   5 □ □ □ □ □ l
                   6 □ □ □ □ □ □ □ □
           7 □ □ □ □ □ □ □ □ □ □
               8     9
          10 □ □ □ □ □ □ □
               □     □
         11 □    □     □
      12 □ □ □ □ □ □    □
      13 □
   14 □ □ □ □ □ □
         □    □
         □    □
```

Answers: page 140

Discussion: 'Fame' Write a list of some people who are currently famous.

Musicians	Actors/Actresses	Sports stars

What do you think are the advantages and disadvantage of being famous?

Advantages	Disadvantages

Compare and discuss your ideas with other people.

David Unaipon

David Unaipon was an inventor and writer. He was the first Aboriginal Australian to write published books. His inventions include a tool for shearing sheep and a new design for a wheel. He also worked hard to make life better for Aboriginal people.

Photo courtesy of State Library of SA. SLSA: B 7326

David Unaipon was born in South Australia, in 1872.

As a young man he loved to read and was interested in science and music. He thought a lot about new ways to fix engineering problems. Between the years 1909 and 1944, David made nine important inventions, including a motor run by centrifugal force. He also made drawings for a helicopter design. He got the idea from the Australian boomerang and the way it moved through the air. This happened in 1914, before we had helicopters.

David lived most of his life in Adelaide and worked for the *Aborigines' Friends Association*. He worked and travelled around south-eastern Australia for fifty years. He often gave talks in schools and churches of different religions about Aboriginal legends and culture, and about his

boomerang

people's future. Sometimes, while travelling from town to town, he was told he couldn't stay in a hotel because he was black, so he understood the problems of racism.

In 1924, Unaipon became the first Aboriginal writer to be published. His most famous book was about Aboriginal legends. His first published writing was an article in Sydney's *Daily Telegraph* newspaper. The article had the title: *'Aboriginals: Their Traditions and Customs'*. He wrote many other articles in newspapers and magazines, getting publicity about the rights of Aboriginal people. He also wrote about the need for co-operation between white and black people, and the need for equal rights for both black and white Australians. He was well educated in both cultures and in 1929 he helped with a government inquiry into Aboriginal health and welfare.

David Unaipon died in 1967 at the age of ninety five, in the same year that Aboriginal people were first counted as part of Australia's population. In 1988, the University of Queensland started the 'David Unaipon Award' which is an award given annually to new Aboriginal writers to help get their books published. The award also honours his achievements in writing, science and Aboriginal welfare.

In 1995, David Unaipon's picture was put on the Australian fifty dollar note.

A) David Unaipon - Vocabulary activity

Find the following words and expressions in the story about David Unaipon
Write them next to their appropriate meaning. The first one has been done as an example.

published books	~~inventor~~ ✓	engineering	annually
shearing sheep	co-operation	helicopter	legends	publicity
equal rights	racism	an article	
welfare	honours	achievements	centrifugal force

1. _____inventor_____ - a person who thinks of new ways to make something or do something

2. _____ - books that are printed and sold for other people to read

3. _____ - cutting the wool from a sheep's skin with special cutters

4. _____ - planning and building bridges, roads and machines

5. _____ - a force that makes things move away from the centre as it

   _____ spins around and around

6. _____ - a flying machine with rotors on top that turn quickly and make it fly

7. _____ - when people are treated badly or unfairly because of their colour or race

8. _____ - stories of a long time ago about places and people of a culture

9. _____ - a short piece of writing in a newspaper or magazine

10. _____ - giving information to many people by newspapers, magazines or presentations

11. _____ - when people work well together

12. _____ - all people allowed to do things or have things equally

13. _____ – the health and living conditions of people in society

14. _____ - happening every year

15. _____ – gives respect and thanks to someone for what they have done

16. _____ – important things that a person plans and does successfully

Answers: page 141

B) David Unaipon - Comprehension activity

Re-read the story about David Unaipon and answer the questions.
Work in a group. One person should read aloud each question below.
Discuss the answer to each question together before you write anything.

1) David Unaipon was the first Aboriginal person to do what?

_____

2) What was his most famous book about?

_____

3) Where can we find a picture of David Unaipon?

_____

4) When and where was he born?

_____

5) As a young man, what was he interested in?

_____

6) What were some of his inventions?

_____   _____

_____   _____

7) Where did he get the idea for his drawings of a helicopter?

_____

8) What did he talk about in schools and churches?

_____

9) What did he write about in magazines and newspaper articles?

_____

10) What is the 'David Unaipon Award'?

_____

Answers: page 141

See group speaking activities on pages 116 – 120.

See a biography writing activity on page 121.

C) Language activities- prepositions

- Prepositions are words such as: in, on, under, over, before, after, about, at, from, for.
- Prepositions show the relationship between nouns (or pronouns) and the other words in the sentence. They often show information about 'where', 'what' and 'when'.

Read the following sentences and highlight the prepositions.

1) Shearers take wool off sheep.   2. Helicopters can fly below the clouds.
3) He was born in South Australia in 1872.   4) He thought a lot about science.

Using the correct preposition

In English, particular prepositions must be used with particular expressions to sound natural.

For example, in the sentence, 'Don't worry <u>about</u> it', the preposition 'about' is the only appropriate preposition to use after 'worry' in this sentence.

The following sentences have been taken from the story about David Unaipon.
Add prepositions to the sentences. You can use the prepositions in the box more than once.

about	into	in	with	of	from	to	between	for	on

1) David Unaipon was the first Aboriginal person in Australia to write published books. His most famous book was _____ Aboriginal legends.

2) As a young man, he loved to read and was very interested _____ science and music.
   He thought a lot _____ new ways to fix engineering problems.

3) David lived most _____ his life in Adelaide and worked _____ the 'Aborigines Friends' Association'.

4) He worked and travelled around south-eastern Australia _____ fifty years and often gave talks in schools and churches of different religions _____ Aboriginal legends.

5) Sometimes, while travelling _____ town _____ town, he was told he couldn't stay in a hotel because he was black, so he understood the problems _____ racism.

6) He also wrote _____ the need for co-operation _____ white and black people, and the need _____ equal rights for both black and white Australians.

7) He worked very hard to make life better _____ Aboriginal people.

8) In 1929, he helped _____ a government inquiry _____ Aboriginal health and welfare.

9) In 1995, David Unaipon's picture was put _____ the Australian $50 note.

Answers: page 141

Adverbs of frequency

Adverbs add meaning to verbs. When we want to say <u>how often</u> something happens or how often we do things, we can choose from the following adverbs:

100%	adverbs	other ways of saying 'how often'
100% ↑	always	all the time, continually (repeated many times or without stopping)
	usually	regularly, on a regular basis, generally, most of the time, on most occasions
	frequently	often, happening a lot, happening many times
	sometimes	now and then, on some occasions but not always
	occasionally	once in a while, from time to time, not regularly
	rarely	hardly ever, not much, almost never happening
0 % ↓	never	not on any occasion, at no time

Other adverbs that tell us how often are:

hourly (happening every hour)   monthly   (happening every month)

daily   (happening every day)   quarterly (happening every three months)

weekly (happening every week)   annually (happening every year or yearly)

Practice with adverbs of frequency

Highlight expressions in the sentences about David Unaipon that show how often things happened.

1. He thought a lot about new ways to fix engineering problems.
2. He often gave talks in schools and churches of different religions about Aboriginal legends.
3. Sometimes, while travelling from town to town, he was told he couldn't stay in a hotel because he was black.
4. The 'David Unaipon Award' is an award given annually to new Aboriginal writers.

Write the adverbs next to their meaning below. Then write them in the crossword on page 75.

Adverb   **Meaning**

1) _____occasionally_____   happening once in a while, not regularly

2) _____   happening all the time

3) _____   happening at no time

4) _____   happening regularly, most of the time

5) _____   happening on some occasions, now and then

6) _____   hardly ever happening, almost never happening

7) _____   happening every year

8) _____   happening often or many times

9) _____   happening every three months

10) _____   happening every week

11) _____   happening every hour

12) _____   happening every month   Answers, page 142

Adverbs of frequency – spelling practice

Write the **adverbs** you have written on page 74 next to the corresponding numbers in the crossword. One has been done as an example.

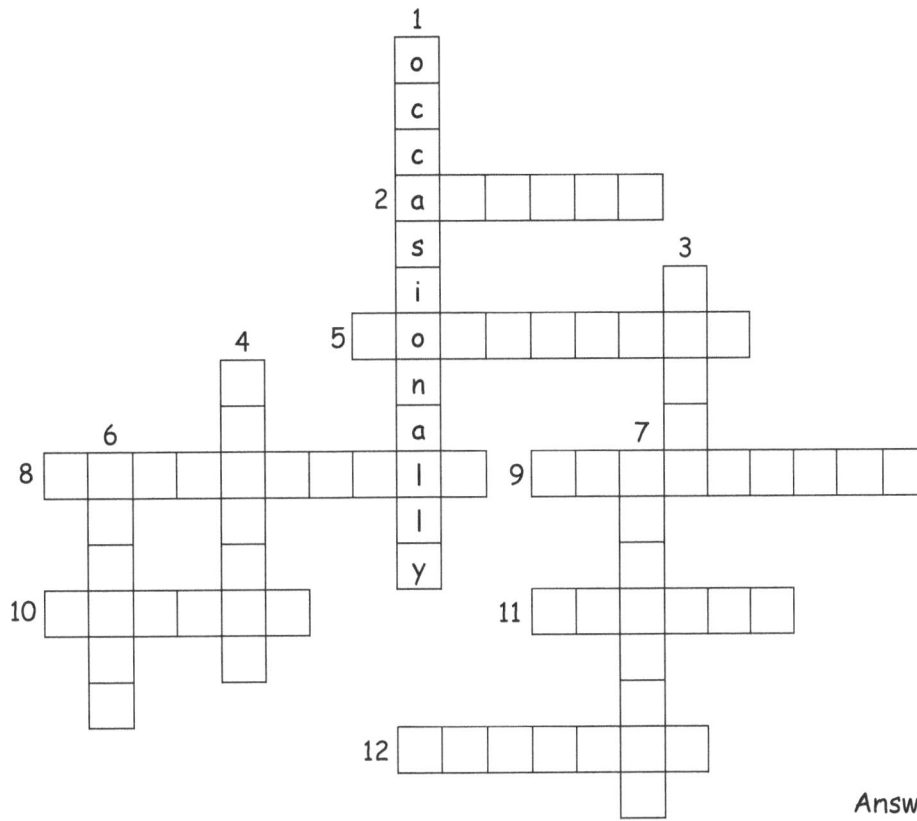

```
                    1
                    o
                    c
                    c
                2   a □ □ □ □ □
                    s              3
                    i              □
            4   5   o □ □ □ □ □ □ □
            □       n              □
        6           a              7
    8   □ □ □ □ □ □ l □ □   9 □ □ □ □ □ □ □ □ □ □
        □           l              □
    10  □ □ □ □ □    y         11  □ □ □ □ □ □
        □                          □
        □                          □
                12  □ □ □ □ □ □ □ □ □
```

Answers: page 142

Discussion

Inventions

Make a list of inventions or discoveries, made during the past 100 years.

Do you know who invented or discovered the things on your list?

In your opinion, which invention has been the most useful?

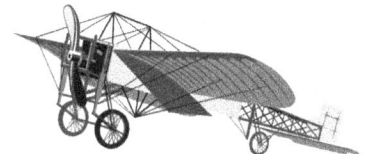

Racism

Discuss the following questions:

What is 'racism'? What causes racism?

Do you agree or disagree with the following statement?

'Education can prevent racism.'

What do **you** think could help to stop or reduce racism?

Share your ideas with other people.

Charles Kingsford Smith

Kingsford Smith was a famous Australian pilot. He made record-breaking flights around Australia, across the Pacific Ocean, to England, and around the world. He began one of Australia's first airlines.

Charles Kingsford Smith was born in Brisbane in 1897. When he was thirteen, he began studying mechanics at college. At the age of eighteen, he joined the army and became a soldier in the First World War. He was sent to fight in France, Egypt and Gallipoli. Later, he joined a new unit of the British Forces that would fly planes for the first time.

Kingsford Smith enjoyed flying planes, which were very simple compared to the planes of today. The planes then were made of wood, fabric and wire. They were difficult and dangerous to fly and had open cockpits so the pilots were exposed to bad weather. During the war, while he was flying, he was shot in the foot when his plane was attacked. As a result, several of his toes were amputated. This injury ended his career in the British Air Force. He was only twenty years old but he was awarded the 'Military Cross', which was a medal to reward his courage.

He then went to America, where he worked as a stunt pilot in Hollywood movies for several years. The movie industry was just beginning and the work was very dangerous but Charles thought it was exciting and it gave him the opportunity to fly planes. However, he quit after someone died during a dangerous stunt.

He returned to Australia and joined 'West Australian Airways'. He flew planes thousands of kilometres across Australia, delivering mail and supplies to country towns. In 1927, he completed an around-Australia flight in ten days and five hours. This was half the time it had taken earlier pilots. It was during this time that he began to focus on his major flying goal; to fly across the Pacific Ocean, the world's largest ocean.

In May 1928, he made the first flight across the Pacific Ocean from the United States to Australia in his plane, the 'Southern Cross'. A few months after that, he made the first non-stop flight across Australia, from Melbourne to Perth. In September, he made the first flight between Australia and New Zealand. One year after that, he made a flight from Australia to England, and set a new record of twelve days and eighteen hours. In 1930, Kingsford Smith began his own airline, 'Australian National Airways', with his friend Charles Ulm, and began flying with passengers.

In 1935, while trying to break another world record, he disappeared while flying between India and Singapore and was never seen again. His picture was on the Australian twenty dollar note until 1994, when a new twenty dollar note was designed. He was given the title 'Sir Charles Kingsford Smith' for his contribution to aviation. Sydney's international airport, 'Sydney Kingsford Smith Airport' was named after him.

A) Charles Kingsford Smith - vocabulary activity

Find and highlight the following words in the story about Charles Kingsford Smith
Write them next to their appropriate meaning.

~~pilot~~ ✓	mechanics	record-breaking	amputated	exposed
cockpits	medal	courage	stunt	to focus
major	goal	contribution	aviation	

1) _____pilot_____ – a person who flies a plane   Answers: page 142

2) _____ - doing or recording something better than anyone or anything else before

3) _____ - the study of machines and how they move and work

4) _____ - the part of a plane where pilots sit and operate the controls

5) _____ - having no cover or protection from the weather

6) _____ - cut off from the body as part of a medical operation

7) _____ - small, metal object, given as a prize for doing something special

8) _____ - to be in a dangerous situation but not be afraid, to be brave

9) _____ - a dangerous act that is done to entertain people, especially in movies

10) _____ - to make something the centre of your attention

11) _____ - the most important or main thing

12) _____ - something you want to do successfully in the future, an aim

13) _____ - something that a person gives or does to help a situation

14) _____ - everything related to flying planes and other aircraft

Early aviation:

The following sketches show side views of planes flown before 1920.

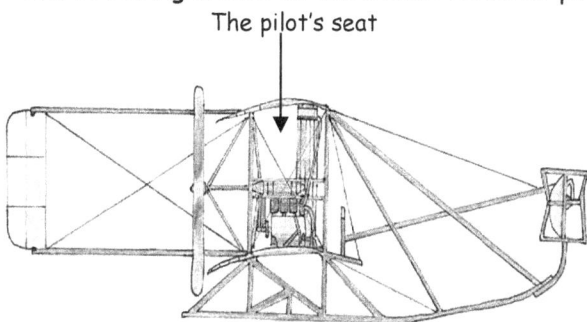

The pilot's seat   The pilot's seat

Sketches by Adam Bagley

Wright 'Flyer' single-seater Biplane (1907-09)
It had one water-cooled 4-cylinder
30-40 h.p. engine and a one-man crew.

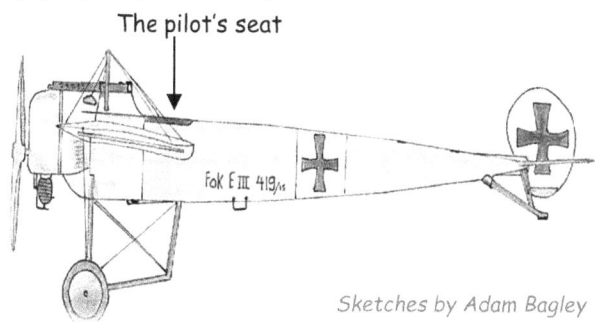

Fokker E-III (M14) Fighter Monoplane (1915-16)
It had one air-cooled rotary 100 h.p. engine
and a one-man crew.

B) Charles Kingsford Smith - Comprehension activity

Work in a group. One person should read aloud each question below.
Discuss the answer to each question before writing anything. Answers, page 143

1) Who was Charles Kingsford Smith?

_____

2) What did he study at college?

_____

3) What did he do when he was eighteen?

_____

4) Why was flying difficult in the early days?

_____

5) What happened when he was twenty years old that ended his job in the British Air Force?

_____

6) What job did he do for several years after his injury?

_____

7) What did he do in 1927?

_____

8) What did he do in the following years:

1928: _____

_____

_____

1929: _____

1930: _____

9) What happened in 1935?_____

_____

10) How was Kingsford Smith awarded and remembered for his contribution to aviation?

_____

C) Language activities – paragraphs

When we write about a topic we use sentences. Then we group the sentences together into paragraphs. Each paragraph starts on a new line and has at least one sentence. Each paragraph has a main topic or idea.

Look at the story about Kingsford Smith on page 76 How many paragraphs are there? Write a number next to each paragraph before you do the following activity.

Practice: Choose the main idea of each paragraph in the Kingsford Smith story.

The main idea of paragraph 1 is: Answers: page 143

    a) where Australia is located
    b) where the Pacific ocean is located
    c) who Kingsford Smith was

The main idea of paragraph 2 is:

    a) the First World War
    b) the planes
    c) Kingsford Smith's early life

The main idea of paragraph 3 is:

    a) the weather
    b) Kingsford Smith's flying experiences during the war
    c) small planes

The main idea of paragraph 4 is:

    a) Kingsford Smith's experience in America
    b) travel in America
    c) movies

The main idea of paragraph 5 is:

    a) Kingsford Smith's flying experiences around Australia
    b) country towns
    c) the Pacific Ocean

The main idea of paragraph 6 is:

    a) Kingsford Smith's airline
    b) Kingsford Smith in New Zealand
    c) Kingsford Smith's flying achievements

The main idea of paragraph 7 is:

    a) Kingsford Smith's disappearance and how he's remembered
    b) Australian $20 note
    c) Sydney Kingsford Smith Airport

In 1928, Kingsford Smith's **Southern Cross** (a Fokker) was the first plane to fly from the United States to Australia across the Pacific, a distance of 11,670 kilometres.

Past tense verbs - review

We add '**d**' or '**ed**' to some verbs for past tense.
 	
            Present   Past
For example: walk ⟶   walk<u>ed</u>
              play ⟶   play<u>ed</u>
 	
Past tense verbs ending in 'ed' are called
regular past **tense**
	We change the spelling of some verbs for past tense.
	
	            Present Past
	For example: do ⟶ did
	              see ⟶ saw
	
	These past tense verbs are **irregular** past **tense**.

Highlight all the past tense verbs in the story about Charles Kingsford Smith.
Write some examples in the correct columns below. Answers: page 143

regular past tense verbs	irregular past tense verbs

Active and passive verbs

Verbs can be active or passive.

How we use active verbs
 	
Active verbs focus on the **subject** of the sentence. This means active verbs focus on the person, organisation or thing **doing the action**.
 	
     subject active
              verb
        ↓
eg. The army <u>sent</u> Kingsford Smith to France.
    The army (subject of the sentence) did the action.
	How we use passive verbs
	
	Passive verbs focus on the person or thing **affected by the action**. The person or thing affected by the action becomes the subject of the sentence.
	
	  subject passive verb
	    ↓
	Kingsford Smith <u>was sent</u> to France by the army.
	Kingsford Smith (subject of the sentence) has the action done to him by the army.

In passive sentences, the person or thing doing the action is not always mentioned.

We **always use past participles** in passive verbs. We form passive sentences in the following ways:

Present simple passive: **singular**   **plural**
                         is + past participle   are + past participle

           eg. My room <u>is cleaned</u> every day.   eg. All the rooms <u>are cleaned</u> every day.

Past simple passive: **singular**   **plural**
                         was + past participle   were + past participle

           eg. My room <u>was cleaned</u> yesterday   eg. All the rooms <u>were cleaned</u> yesterday.

Future passive: **singular**   **plural**
                         will be + past participle   will be + past participle

           eg. My room <u>will be cleaned</u> tomorrow.   eg. All the rooms <u>will be cleaned</u> tomorrow.

     *See a list of verbs, showing past participles online at <u>www.boyereducation.com.au</u>
     Click on 'Free Resources' for a PDF download 'Information about English Verbs'.

Active and passive verbs - practice

Practice 1) Find and highlight <u>ten passive verbs</u> in the following sentences about Kingsford Smith.

At the age of eighteen, he joined the army and became a soldier in the First World War. He was sent to fight in France, Egypt and Gallipoli. Later, he joined a new unit of the British Forces that would fly planes for the first time.

The planes then were made of wood, fabric and wire. They were difficult and dangerous to fly and had open cockpits so the pilots were exposed to bad weather.

During the war, he was shot in the foot when his plane was attacked. As a result, several of his toes were amputated. This injury ended his career in the British Air Force. He was only twent y years old but he was awarded the 'Military Cross', which was a medal to reward his courage.

His picture was on the Australian $20 note until 1994, when a new $20 note was designed. He was given the title 'Sir Charles Kingsford Smith' for his contribution to aviation. Sydney's international airport, 'Sydney Kingsford Smith Airport' was named after him.

In a passive sentence, the person or thing doing the action is often not mentioned.
When the person or thing doing the action is mentioned, we generally use '**by**' to introduce them.

For example:
subject   passive verb   person doing the action
The rooms were cleaned by Chris.

Practice 2) Change the following sentences to passive. One has been done as an example.

Active sentence	Passive sentence
1. The army sent Kingsford Smith to France.	_Kingsford Smith was sent to France._
2. Manufacturers made the first planes with wood and wire.	_____
3. The open cockpits exposed the pilots to bad weather.	_____
4. The enemy attacked his plane.	_____
5. Doctors amputated several of Kingsford Smith's toes.	_____
6. The army awarded Kingsford Smith a medal.	_____
7. The government gave him the title 'Sir Kingsford Smith'.	_____
8. They named Sydney's international airport after him.	_____

Answers: page 143

Sydney Kingsford Smith Airport is one of the oldest continually operated airports in the world.

John Flynn

John Flynn is famous because he started the Royal Flying Doctor Service of Australia. This was the world's first air ambulance service to provide emergency transport and emergency medical attention for people in outback Australia.

John Flynn was born in 1880, in a small town, in Victoria. His mother died when he was three so he spent much of his childhood living with relatives. When he left school in 1898 he worked as a schoolteacher. However, in 1903 he decided to become a Christian minister and began visiting small towns in remote areas of Victoria, South Australia, Queensland and the Northern Territory. He saw the urgent need for health care for people living in the vast Australian outback. He heard many sad stories of sick people dying before they could get to a hospital. He wanted to help the isolated communities of inland Australia so he began a magazine called *The Inlander*. He used photographs, maps and true stories in his magazine to show the difficulties of white and aboriginal communities living far from medical help. He used his magazine to make known his plans and to raise money so he could set up simple 'bush hospitals' in small outback towns.

By 1917, Flynn began thinking about using new technology such as radio communication and an air ambulance service to get urgent medical help to people in the outback. In 1920, he wrote about his idea of having a 'flying doctor' service which was an amazing idea in those days. By 1928, he had raised enough money to begin using small planes to fly doctors and nurses to emergency situations. In its first year, the service flew fifty flights, becoming the first air ambulance service in the world.

In 1929, the first 'pedal radio' was made using bicycle pedals to drive a generator and Flynn used the idea to set up a communication network for outback communities. In 1933, he received an award called 'Order of the British Empire'. His picture is on the Australian twenty dollar note with a picture of the first QANTAS plane used by the organisation. Sadly, John Flynn died of cancer in 1951.

Today, the Royal Flying Doctor Service is still used across 7,000,000 square kilometres or 80% of the Australian continent. Eighty percent of medical emergencies in Australia's outback are attended by only a nurse and pilot while a doctor gives instructions to the nurse from a medical centre far away.

The Royal Flying Doctor Service continues to be the largest emergency 'flying' health care service in the world.

A) John Flynn - Vocabulary activity

Find the following words and expressions in the story about **John Flynn** and write them next to their appropriate meaning. The first one has been done as an example.

~~outback~~ ✓	urgent need	minister	remote	vast	isolated communities

radio communication   set up   pedal radio   generator   pilot

award   continent   communication network   QANTAS

1. _____outback_____ - places were few people live, far away from town and cities

2. _____ – a person who works for a Christian church

3. _____ – very far away from cities and city services

4. _____ – when help is needed as soon as possible, immediately

5. _____ – very, very large (to describe an area)

6. _____ – people living far away from other people and services

7. _____ – organise an activity or the building of something

8. _____ – using radio to send and receive messages from other people

9. _____ - making power for radio by pedalling with the feet (see picture below)

10. _____ – a machine that makes electricity

11. _____ – people and places linked by radio or other ways of communication

12. _____ – a prize for doing something special

13. _____ – Queensland and Northern Territory Aerial Services

14. _____ – one of the earth's very large areas of land

15. _____ – person who flies a plane

The photograph shows a man using a 'pedal wireless' in 1930.

Answers: page 144

B) John Flynn - Comprehension activity

Re-read the story about **John Flynn** and answer the questions.
Work in a group. One person should read aloud each question below.
Discuss the answer to each question together before you write anything.

1) Why is John Flynn famous?

_____

2) What did he do in 1903?

_____

3) What did he see and hear in the Australian outback?

_____

4) Why did he start a magazine called *The Inlander*?

_____

5) What idea did he write about in 1920?

_____

6) When did John Flynn begin using planes to fly doctors to medical emergencies?

_____

7) In 1929, what did he use to improve communication for outback communities?

_____

8) Where can we see a picture of John Flynn?

_____

9) Where does the Flying Doctor Service operate now?

_____

10) What do the letters R.F.D.S. on the sign below mean?

_____

Answers: page 144

C) Language activities – Adjectives review

Adjectives describe and give more information about people and things.
Highlight the adjectives in the sentences about John Flynn in the box below:

John Flynn saw the urgent need for health care for people living in the Australian outback.
He wanted to help the isolated communities of inland Australia. In 1920, he wrote about his
idea of having a 'flying doctor' service which was an amazing idea in those days.

The service he began in 1928 continues to be the largest 'air ambulance' service in the world.

Answers page: 144.

Adjectives with special suffixes

A suffix is a letter or group of letters added to the end of words to make a special meaning.
Adjectives ending in 'ed' describe people or things **affected by a situation or feeling**.

1) Some adjectives end with '**ed**'. Examples are: a <u>bored</u> child, a <u>tired</u> dog, <u>interested</u> students.

Find an example in the sentences in the box above about John Flynn? _____

Adjectives ending in 'ing' describe **things (or people) that cause a feeling.**

2) Some adjectives end with '**ing**'. Examples are: a <u>boring</u> movie, a <u>tiring</u> walk, an <u>interesting</u> lesson.

Find an example in the sentences in the box above about John Flynn? _____

3) Some adjectives end in '**est**'. Examples are: the <u>oldest</u> building, the <u>highest</u> mountain
These words are called superlative adjectives and are used to describe something with '**the most
of a particular quality**'. Find an example in the box above about John Flynn?_____

Abbreviations and acronyms

An **abbreviation** is a shortened form of a word.
For example, we write 'Rd' as an abbreviation of 'Road'.

An **acronym** is made by using the first letter of other words.
WHO is an acronym for <u>W</u>orld <u>H</u>ealth <u>O</u>rganisation.

An acronym is a type of abbreviation.
What do the following acronyms mean?

Write all the words.   Answers, page 144

QANTAS _____

_____

NAIDOC _____

ANZAC _____

What other acronyms do you know?

_____   _____

What other abbreviations do you know?

_____   _____

Examples of abbreviations are:		
Tues	=	Tuesday
Aust.	=	Australia
gov.	=	government
e.g.	=	for example
km	=	kilometre
dept.	=	department

Synonyms

A synonym is a word, expression or phrase with a similar meaning to another word or phrase. For example, the word 'little' is a synonym of 'small'. These words have a similar meaning.

The words in the box below have been taken from the text about John Flynn.

~~remote~~ ✓	famous	true	largest	far	provide	began	urgent
difficulties	vast	amazing	sad	new	enough		

The words in the box above can be used as synonyms for the words in the following list.

Write a **synonym** from the box to show the meaning of the following words.   Answers, page 144

Write the **Synonyms**

1. far away _____ *remote* _____

2. biggest _____

3. give, supply _____

4. a long way _____

5. well known _____

6. surprising _____

7. huge, immense _____

8. started _____

9. immediately necessary _____

10. unhappy _____

11. sufficient _____

12. problems _____

13. factual _____

14. recently made _____

A **dictionary** uses synonyms to explain the meaning of words.

e.g. **remote** *adj.* far away; isolated

A **thesaurus** is a reference book in which words are put into groups with other words or phrases with similar meanings.

e.g. **remote** *adj.*
    distant; far away; far off; secluded; far removed; lonely; isolated; out of the way.

You can increase your vocabulary by using a dictionary or thesaurus.

Write the synonyms you wrote above in the crossword next to the corresponding numbers. One has been done as an example.

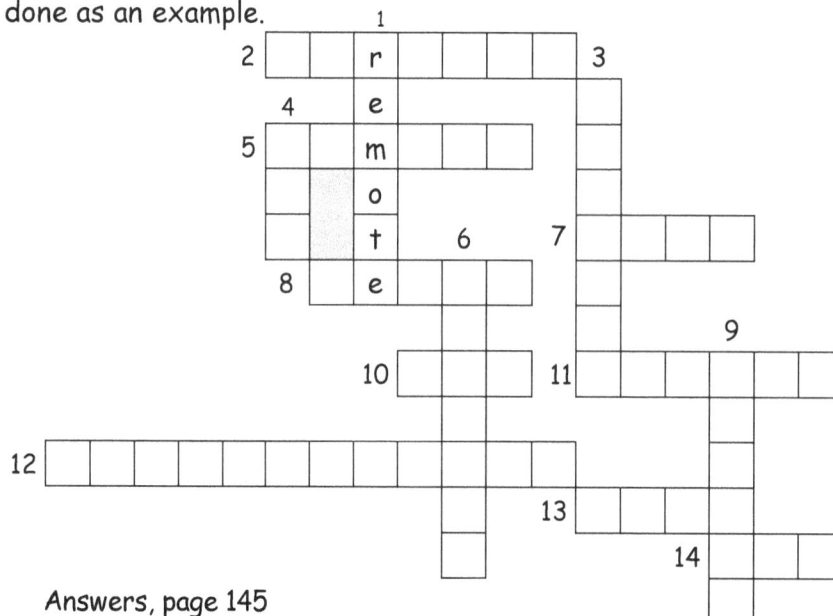

Answers, page 145

Expressing meaning with words or numbers

Written texts often include numbers to show information such as amounts, percentages or dates.

Guidelines for writing and saying numbers:

In stories, years are usually written numerically. For example: John Flynn was born in **1880**. However, we generally read years in the following way: John Flynn was born in **eighteen eighty**.

- Usually when saying a year number we say it in two parts:

For example: 1951 is read as ̂nineteen ̂fifty-one.

The year **2019** is read as ̂twenty ̂nineteen or as ̂two thousand and ̂nineteen

- In writing, numbers over 100 are usually written with numbers, eg. 7,000,000 square kilometres However, if preferred, they can be written with words, eg. seven million square kilometres

- Percentages can be written as numbers or words. For example: 10% or 'ten per cent' 'One percent' means: 'one part of one hundred parts'.

  So, **'one per cent'** can be shown as **1%** or as **'one hundredth'** or as a fraction $\frac{1}{100}$.

- Ordinal numbers, which show the order of things, can be written with numbers(**1st**, **2nd**, **3rd**) or with words (**first, second, third**). However, in written stories we generally use words.

  For example: This was the world's **first** air ambulance service.

Practice: Highlight the references to numerical information in the text about John Flynn below.

By 1928, he had raised enough money to begin using small planes to fly doctors and nurses to emergency situations. In its first year, the service flew fifty flights, becoming the first air ambulance service in the world.

In 1929, the first 'pedal radio' was made using bicycle pedals to drive a generator and Flynn used the idea to set up a communication network for outback communities.

In 1933, he received an award called Order of the British Empire. His picture is on the Australian twenty dollar note with a picture of the first QANTAS plane used by the organisation.

Today, the Royal Flying Doctor Service is still used across 7,000,000 square kilometres, or 80% of the Australian continent. Eighty percent of medical emergencies in Australia's outback are attended by only a nurse and pilot while a doctor gives instructions to the nurse from a medical centre far away. The Royal Flying Doctor Service continues to be the largest emergency 'flying' health care service in the world.

Answers, page 145

Discussion – Health and communication services

In what ways have health services advanced since John Flynn's lifetime?
In what ways have communication services advanced since John Flynn's lifetime?

Find information about a recent invention or new technology that has improved medical treatment. Explain the information to other people.

Douglas Mawson

Douglas Mawson was an adventurer and a geologist. He explored large areas of Antarctica and made one of the greatest contributions to the world's knowledge of the weather, geology and wildlife of the Antarctic continent.

Douglas Mawson was born in England and in 1884 came to Australia with his family as a two year old boy. At school he was interested in geology and later studied mining engineering at the University of Sydney. In 1905, he became a lecturer at the University of Adelaide and three years later he joined explorers on a British Antarctic Expedition to do scientific research in Antarctica.

After crossing the Southern Ocean to Antarctica, the explorers set up a base camp and began scientific testing of the weather and life in the icy sea. In September that year, Mawson was part of a team that left the base camp for a journey of 2028 kilometres to reach the magnetic South Pole. Mawson's team faced many dangers. Blizzards, snow blindness and frostbite made their journey painful and they had to take care not to fall into deep ice crevasses. After months of difficulty, they reached the magnetic South Pole in early 1909. They took photos and raised the British flag to claim the area for Britain. Then they pulled their sledges 2028 kilometres back to the base camp.

After returning to Australia, Mawson organised equipment and men for his own 'Australasian Antarctic Expedition'. The expedition set off by ship in December 1911. Firstly, they set up a communication base on Macquarie Island, 1300 kilometres south east of Tasmania, so that the first wireless radio signals could be sent to the world from Antarctica. Then they headed across the Southern Ocean to the Antarctic continent to do scientific research and chart the Antarctic coastline directly south of Australia.

They reached Cape Denison in January 1912 and set up a base camp. It was one of the coldest, windiest places on the earth but it was full of wildlife such as seals and penguins. Through March and April the wind speed ranged from 100 to 300 kms per hour. It took them five months to build a communication tower due to the extreme weather. However, the first radio signals were successfully sent from Antarctica to Macquarie Island before the tower blew down.

By November, the weather had improved so Mawson and two other men, Mertz and Ninnis, set out to do more exploring with sledges pulled by dogs. They travelled east for 500 kms, collecting geological samples. In December while crossing ice, Ninnis fell into a deep crevasse and was never seen again. As well as losing their friend, they lost a sledge, six dogs, their tent and most of their food and clothing. They began the journey back to the main camp but became so hungry they had to eat the remaining dogs. After twenty-five days on the return journey, Mertz, who was exhausted and sick, also died. Mawson struggled on alone for another thirty days. He was weak and starving but he managed to carry the scientific records and samples of his journey more than 160 kms across ice and snow. When he reached the main camp, he was almost dead.

When he returned to Australia, he was greeted as a hero and was given the title of 'Sir Douglas Mawson' for his great Antarctic exploration and research. 'Mawson Station', Australia's main base in Antarctica, is named after him.

A) Douglas Mawson - Vocabulary activity

Find the following words and expressions in the story about Douglas Mawson and write them next to the appropriate meaning. The first one has been done as an example.

explored	blizzards	~~geologist~~ ✓	expedition	a base camp
snow blindness	journey	contribution	magnetic South Pole	frostbite
sledges	crevasses	extreme	chart	hero	geological samples

1. _____geologist_____ - a person who studies rocks and the earth's surface

2. _____ - searched for new things that had not been seen or known before

3. _____ - something given to help other people or to make something successful

4. _____ - an organised trip to a place with a group of people and equipment, etc

5. _____ - a place where food and supplies are kept when doing trips around an area

6. _____ - a trip, when you travel a long way to another place

7. _____ - the place on the Earth which a compass shows as south, opposite to north

8. _____ - storms with snow and very strong wind

9. _____ - not able to see anything because of the brightness of the snow

10. _____ - when very cold weather gives pain and damages fingers and toes

11. _____ - very deep, long holes in ice-covered areas

12. _____ - vehicles to travel on snow, with long pieces of metal instead of wheels

13. _____ - make a map or record information about something over a period of time

14. _____ - describing the most serious possible situation

15. _____ - small pieces of something (e.g. rock) to study or show what it looks like

16. _____ - a person who does something very brave and good

Answers: page 145

Mawson, Edgeworth & Mackay raised
the flag at the Magnetic South Pole
on 16 January 1909

B) Douglas Mawson - Comprehension activity

Work in a group. One person should read aloud each question below.
Discuss the answer to each question together before you write anything.

1) Who was Douglas Mawson?

_____

2) What did he contribute to the world?

_____

3) What kind of research did the explorers of the British Antarctic Expedition do in Antarctica?

_____

4) What dangers did Mawson and his team face on their journey to the magnetic South Pole?

_____

5) What did the 'Australasian Antarctic Expedition' do in 1911?

_____

6) What was the weather like at Cape Denison?

_____

7) What did he do with two other men, Mertz and Ninnis?

_____

8) What happened to his friend Ninnis?

_____

9) What happened to his friend, Mertz?

_____

10) How was Mawson greeted when he returned to Australia?

_____

Answers: page 146

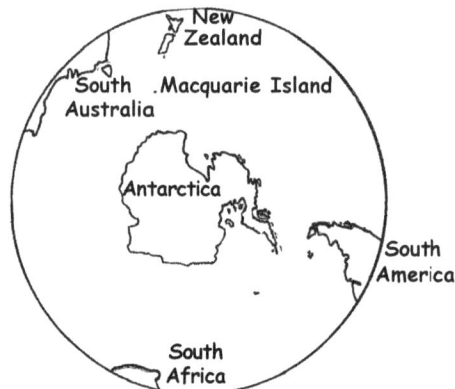

This drawing of the Antarctic region
does not show exact distance or size.

C) The use of 'articles' - a, an, the

Words such as **a**, **an**, **the** are called **articles**. They are used before nouns.
Some examples are: **the** weather, **a** journalist, **an** accident
They are also used before noun groups. For example: **a** two year old boy.

Read the story on page 88 again and **highlight the articles** (a, an, the) in different colours so you can analyse the different ways they are used. Also, highlight the articles in the examples below.

- **A** and **an** are called <u>indefinite articles</u>; we use them with singular nouns.

  We use articles 'a' or 'an':

a) when a person or thing talked or written about isn't unique or specific

  e.g. Mawson came to Australia as <u>a</u> young boy. (Other young boys came to Australia so it isn't unique)
      He was <u>a</u> lecturer at the University of Adelaide. (There were other lecturers at the university.)

b) when something is mentioned for the first time and therefore unfamiliar to the reader or hearer.

  e.g. They set up <u>a</u> base camp. (This is the first time a 'base camp' is mentioned.)

Note: '<u>an</u>' follows the patterns as above but is used before words beginning with a vowel (a, e, i, o, u)
      e.g. Douglas Mawson was <u>an</u> <u>a</u>dventurer. (There have been other adventurers so it is not unique.)

Practice 1 Complete the sentence about Douglas Mawson (page 88, line 12) with **indefinite articles**.

In September that year, Mawson was part of _____ that left the base

camp for_____ of 2028 kilometres to reach the magnetic South Pole.

- '**The**' is called the definite article. It can be used with singular and plural nouns.
  We use the article 'the':

a) when we talk about things that have been mentioned previously in the conversation and are known.

  e.g. <u>The</u> explorers left <u>the</u> base camp for a journey of 2028 kilometres. (The explorers and the base camp were mentioned previously in the story.)

b) when we talk about something unique, definite or specific.

  e.g. They reached <u>the</u> magnetic South Pole. (The magnetic South Pole is unique; there is only one.)
  e.g. They took photos and raised <u>the</u> British flag. (The British flag is unique; it is specific.)

  Note: We say: <u>the</u> earth, <u>the</u> sky, <u>the</u> sun, <u>the</u> moon, <u>the</u> stars, <u>the</u> weather.

c) when we use superlative adjectives. (e.g. the first explorer, the coldest place) ★

  e.g. He made one of <u>the</u> greatest contributions to <u>the</u> world's knowledge of Antarctica.

d) when a place name or place description includes an adjective, 'the' is generally used.

  e.g. <u>the</u> Southern Ocean, <u>the</u> Antarctic continent, <u>the</u> magnetic South Pole
  when titles or phrases include '... of...' e.g. <u>the</u> University <u>of</u> Adelaide, <u>the</u> geology <u>of</u> Antarctica

---

Practice 2 Complete the sentence about Douglas Mawson (page 88, line 27) with **definite articles**.

However, _____ were successfully sent from Antarctica to

Macquarie Island before _____ blew down.

Answers: page 146

Omission of articles

No article is used when talking about things in <u>general, non-specific ways</u>.
   e.g. He was interested in <u>geology</u>. (not ~~the~~ geology)
   However, we would say '<u>the geology of Antarctica</u>' because it is a specific region or type of geology.

   Generally, '**the**' <u>is not used</u> before proper nouns. ie. names of people, places, months, etc
   e.g. They reached Cape Denison in January. (No articles are used in this sentence).
   However, see explanation d) page 91 about when to use 'the' with place names and descriptions.

Practice 3 – using articles correctly

Write the articles **a**, **an** or **the** where you think they should be in the text about Douglas Mawson:
Leave a space where there should be no article.

Douglas Mawson was _____¹ adventurer and _____² geologist He explored large areas of ___³ Antarctica and made one of _____ ⁴ greatest contributions to _____ ⁵ world's knowledge of the weather, geology and wildlife of _____ ⁶ Antarctic continent.

At school, he was interested in ___ ⁷geology and later studied mining engineering at the University of Sydney. In 1905, he became a lecturer at the University of Adelaide and three years later he joined explorers on a British Antarctic Expedition to do scientific research in _____⁸ Antarctica.

After crossing the Southern Ocean to _____⁹ Antarctica, _____ ¹⁰ explorers set up ____¹¹ base camp and began scientific testing of the weather and life in the icy sea. In September that year, Mawson was part of a team that left _____¹² base camp for a journey of 2028 kilometres to reach _____¹³ magnetic South Pole. Mawson's team faced many dangers. After months of difficulty, they reached _____¹⁴ magnetic South Pole in early 1909. They took photos and raised _____¹⁵ British flag to claim the area for Britain. Then they pulled their sledges 2028 kilometres back to _____¹⁶ base camp.

After returning to _____¹⁷Australia, Mawson organised equipment and men for his own 'Australasian Antarctic Expedition'. _____¹⁸ expedition set off by ship in December 1911. Firstly, they set up a communication base on __ ¹⁹ Macquarie Island, 1300 kilometres south east of ___²⁰Tasmania, so that _____ ²¹ first wireless radio signals could be sent to _____ ²² world from Antarctica. It took them five months to build a communication tower due to the extreme weather. However, _____²³ first radio signals were successfully sent from Antarctica to_____ ²⁴ Macquarie Island before _____ ²⁵ tower blew down.

Now check your work. You should have added 14 definite articles and 3 indefinite articles.

Answers: page 146

Phrasal verbs

In English, it is common to use prepositions (in, up, off, on, out) together with verbs to express special meanings. These 'two word verbs' are called **phrasal verbs**.

For example, 'come in' is a phrasal verb meaning 'enter'. 'Come back' means 'return'.

Generally, phrasal verbs have a specific meaning when the verb and preposition are used together and can differ greatly from the meaning of the words used separately.

For example, the words 'turn' and 'up', when used in separate sentences, have a completely different meaning when used together as the phrasal verb 'turn up'.
For example, 'He didn't <u>turn up</u>.' means 'He didn't <u>arrive</u>'.

As there are many phrasal verbs, the meaning of each expression should be learnt in context.

Practice: Read the sentences below. Each sentence has a phrasal verb using the verb 'set'.

Underline the phrasal verb in each sentence.

set in = something unwanted may happen or continue: He thinks the rain has <u>set in</u> for the day.
Infection may set in where the dog bit him.

set up = organise or build something at a place: They set up a company overseas.
He set up cameras for the movie shoot.

set off = start a journey: He set off down the road in his new car.
What time will you set off tomorrow?

set out = begin an action or journey for a specific purpose: He set out to find a cure for cancer.
(<u>set out</u> and <u>set off</u> can have almost the same meaning)   We'll set out for the coast early tomorrow.

Look at the following sentence from the story about Douglas Mawson.
Underline the <u>phrasal verb</u>. What does it mean?   Answers: page 146

1. After taking months to reach Antarctica by ship, the explorers set up a base camp.

Complete the following sentences from Douglas Mawson's story (page 88) with a phrasal verb.

2. The expedition _____ by ship in December 1911. (line 19)

3. Firstly, they _____ a communication base on Macquarie Island. (line 19)

4. They reached Cape Denison in January 1912 and _____ a base camp. (line 24)

5. Mawson and two other men, Mertz and Ninnis, _____ to do more exploring with sledges pulled by dogs. (line 29)

Mawson called Cape Denison
'the windiest place on Earth'
This photo shows a blizzard
there in 1912.

Photograph by Frank Hurley 1912

Vincent Lingiari

Vincent Lingiari was a skilled Aboriginal stockman who became a role-model in the civil rights movement in Australia. He used non-violent ways to fight a long, hard battle for a fair go for his people.

PM Whitlam 'handing back' land to Vincent Lingiari

Vincent Lingiari was born on a cattle station in the Northern Territory in 1919. His people, the Gurindji, had lived there for thousands of years before Europeans arrived with cattle to set up the Wave Hill Station. By the time Vincent was born, the property was run by a wealthy British company and covered thousands of square kilometres. They used the local Aboriginal people as workers, providing food rations and low quality housing as payment. Those who did receive a wage, were paid much less than white workers doing the same job.

Vincent was working on the station by the time he was twelve, and over time he became unhappy with the unfair treatment of his people. In 1966, tired of the exploitation, he went to the manager and asked that his people receive the same payment as white men. The manager's reply was, 'No.' Vincent decided to do something to draw attention to the unjust situation. In August 1966, he led two hundred employees and their families in a peaceful protest. They walked off the Wave Hill property and camped at a nearby creek.

At first, the strike was about better wages and living conditions but it grew into something much bigger. Gradually the idea evolved that the Gurindji should reclaim their land and run their own cattle station rather than working for someone else. They knew they had the skills and knowledge to do it. With support from indigenous and non-indigenous people, their determination grew. With the help of Australian writer Frank Hardy, they wrote a petition to the governor-general. A key point of their letter was: *'We feel that morally the land is ours and should be returned to us.'* They were disappointed when their request was refused, however Vincent Lingiari and his people did not give up. They were determined to continue their strike, believing in their rights.

In 1968 Frank Hardy published a book called 'The Unlucky Australians' which later became a documentary film. This brought international attention and support for the Gurindji struggle. In 1972 newly elected Prime Minister Gough Whitlam announced he would do something about the situation. Progress was slow but finally, in August 1975 - nine years after their strike began – the Gurindji people won their land back. When Prime Minster Whitlam handed over the deeds, he also put a handful of soil into Lingiari's hand, saying:

> 'Vincent Lingiari, I solemnly hand to you these deeds as proof, in Australian law, that these lands belong to the Gurindji people and I put into your hands part of the earth as a sign that this land will be the possession of you and your children forever.'

Lingiari was awarded an Order of Australia (AM) medal in 1977 for what he had achieved for Aboriginal people. With the Gurindji people, he had advanced the land rights movement. He died in 1988 but his inspiring story is told in the song, 'From Little Things Big Things Grow'. *

*Song written by Kev Carmody & Paul Kelly; recorded in 1991.

A) Vincent Lingiari - Vocabulary activity

Find and highlight the following words and expressions in the story about Vincent Lingiari. Write them next to the appropriate meaning. The first one has been done as an example.

~~civil rights movement~~	role model	stockman	food rations	exploitation
strike	evolved	reclaim	determination	petition
morally	rights	solemnly	deeds	

1. ___civil rights movement___ - protests in 1960s to bring justice & social change

2. _____ - a person who is admired and looked to as an example to be followed

3. _____ - a person whose job is to look after livestock such as cattle

4. _____ - abuse and misuse of someone

5. _____ - fixed allowance or amount of food

6. _____ - developed and grew into something different

7. _____ - get something back that once belonged to you

8. _____ - a refusal to work as a protest of bad conditions

9. _____ - a formal written request to someone in authority

10. _____ - honestly, justly, properly, decently

11. _____ - fair, honest and correct claims of all humans for fair treatment

12. _____ - a signed paper giving ownership of property or legal rights

13. _____ - in a serious, respectful and sincere way

Answers, page 147

Gurindji stockmen proudly assembled near the sign to their cattle station (photo by Brian Manning 1967)

B) Vincent Lingiari - Comprehension activity

Work in a group. One person should read aloud each question below.
Discuss the answer to each question together before you write anything.

1) Who was Vincent Lingiari?

_____

2) When and where was he born?

_____

3) What happened in August 1966?

_____

4) What did the Gurindji people ask the governor-general in a petition and what was the result?

_____

_____

5) How did writer Frank Hardy support the Gurindji people?

_____

6) What happened in the following years?

1972: _____

1975: _____

1977: _____

7) Read the following sentences and highlight the correct underlined words:

The Gurindji people live in the <u>Northern Territory</u> / <u>Queensland</u>, In 1883, Wave Hill Station, was set up on their land approximately 600 kilometres <u>south</u> / <u>north</u> of Darwin. In <u>1965</u> / <u>1975</u> their land was returned to them.

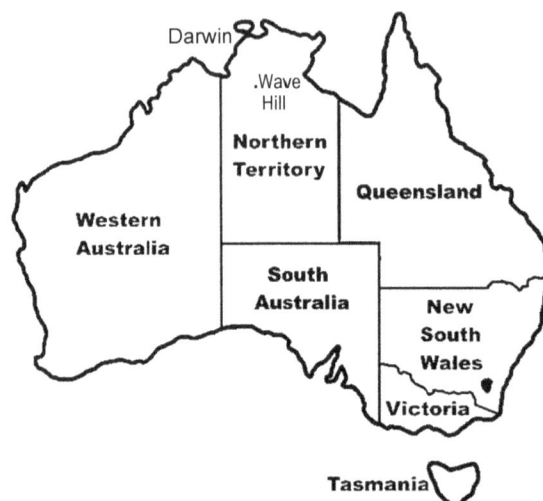

Answers: page 147

C) Language activity – Punctuation

'Punctuation' means the written symbols or marks that provide additional help in understanding written texts. You can see a list of pronunciation symbols on page 98.

Quotation marks are a set of punctuation symbols used to show the beginning and end of direct speech in a written text. Direct speech means the exact words that someone said.
Quotation marks can be shown as single '   ' marks, or double "   " marks.
In general, British English uses single quotation marks; American English uses double quotation marks.

Quotation marks are generally used to show titles such as:

• the title of a book, e.g. This book is called 'People in Australia's Past'.
• chapter titles in a book, e.g. 'Bennelong' is one of the stories in 'People in Australia's Past'.
• the name of a play or movie, e.g. The movie 'The Sound of Music' was produced in 1965.
• the title of a song or a music album, e.g. 'Jailhouse Rock' was a popular song by Elvis Presley.
• a direct quote from another person's writing such as an essay, report, book or letter,
   e.g. In his report he stated, 'All work will be finished by the end of the year.'

Practice:

Find and highlight five examples of quotation marks in Vincent Lingiari's story, page 94.

Now add quotation marks in the correct places to sections from Lingiari's story below:

1) **A quote from a letter**:

   With the help of Australian writer Frank Hardy, they wrote a petition to the governor- general.
   A key point in their letter was: We feel that morally the land is ours and should be returned to us.

2) **The title of a book**:

   In 1968, Frank Hardy published a book called The Unlucky Australians which later became a
   documentary film.

3) **Words of a speech** (words that someone said):

   When Prime Minster Whitlam handed over the deeds, he put a handful soil into Lingiari's hand,
   saying: Vincent Lingiari, I solemnly hand to you these deeds as proof, in Australian law, that
         these lands belong to the Gurindji people and I put into your hands part of the earth
         as a sign that this land will be the possession of you and your children forever.

4) **The title of a song**:

   Lingiari had advanced the Aboriginal land rights movement...his inspiring story is told in the song,
   From Little Things Big Things Grow.

Answers page 147

While Frank Hardy was researching his book, 'The Unlucky Australians' he made a drawing of Vincent Lingiari in a field book.

His drawing, 'Vincent - May 1968' was shown at the National Library of Australia's '1968 Changing Times' exhibition in 2018.

VINCENT
may 68

D) Punctuation symbols.

Look at the following table for the names, uses and examples of punctuation symbols:

Punctuation mark	Name	Uses	Example
A B C D E F	capital letters	• the first letter of a new sentence • the first letter of names of days, people, cities, countries, etc (for more information, see page 51) • for acronyms and abbreviations	A storm began suddenly. Sunday David Australia QANTAS, Dr, USA
.	full stop (also 'period')	• at the end of a written sentence • sometimes after an abbreviation	We went for a walk today. Mr. and Mrs. Jones
?	question mark	• at the end of a written question	What is your name?
!	exclamation mark	• at the end of a sentence that shows surprise or shock • to indicate a shout or loud noise	That is amazing! Oh no! Stop! Help! Crash!
,	comma	• after items on a list • between adjectives written before a noun (but not with 'and') • to divide a long sentence, to show a pause • before a question tag	I'll buy tea, coffee, cake, sugar and milk. The ground was hot, dry, hard and barren. The meeting is after lunch, so I'll wait till it's finished. It is cold, isn't it?
'	apostrophe	• to show missing letter in contractions • for possessives, to show ownership	I'm-don't-haven't-we'll-it's David's car my friend's boat
:	colon	• to introduce lists or relate information • sometimes before a direct quotation	You will need the following: paper, glue, pencils, folder. He said: 'You're correct!'
;	semi colon	• to separate related information in formal writing	Nothing could be done; it was too late.
-	hyphen	• to join two or more words that form a new meaning	mother-in-law middle-aged
( )	brackets (also called parentheses)	• used within a sentence to include extra information or an example.	He ran four kilometres (two and a half miles) without stopping once.
" " or ' '	quotation marks (also called inverted commas)	• to show the beginning and end of direct speech in a story • to quote another person' s writing or show another person originally wrote or spoke the words	He said, 'Sorry I'm late.' Wilson announced, 'If you believe, it will happen.'

Punctuation symbols

Write the names of the punctuation symbols below. The first has been done as an example.
Complete the crossword by writing the names of the symbols next to the corresponding numbers.

	name		symbol
1.	_____ full stop _____		.
2.	_____ _____		A
3.	_____		,
4.	_____		:
5.	_____ _____		!
6.	_____		-
7.	_____		,
8.	_____ _____		;
9.	_____ _____		?
10.	_____		( )
11.	_____ _____		' '

Crossword grid:

1 down: f u l l s t o p

Answers: page 147

Oodgeroo Noonuccal (Kath Walker)

Oodgeroo Noonuccal was a famous Australian poet, author, and educator. She began writing as Kath Walker but later changed her name to Oodgeroo to represent her Aboriginal heritage. She believed poems and stories could draw attention to the injustice facing her people.

Kath was born in 1920 on Stradbroke Island, off the coast of Queensland, near Brisbane. She spent her childhood fishing and playing on the sand hills after school, or horse-riding with her father when his workday finished. However, she was aware of racial inequality on the island because Aboriginal people were not allowed to sit in the same cinema seats as the Europeans who worked on the island.

Although she was a clever, creative student she left school at the age of thirteen and began doing domestic work in Brisbane. She was paid less for her work than white Australian women doing the same job. From an early age, she believed these issues should be addressed.

During World War 2, she volunteered for the *Australian Women's Army Service* performing various office duties. Then, when she was twenty-two, she married a childhood friend, Bruce Walker. Over the following decade, while raising two sons, she became involved in the civil rights movement.

In 1962, as part of a delegation, she met with Prime Minister Menzies to discuss when Aboriginal people would be counted as part of Australia's national census. During this time she also wrote poems about the injustice faced by her people and her hope for a fairer future. In the 1962 meeting, she read her poem called 'Aboriginal Charter of Rights', and it made a big impact. Her first book of poems was published in 1964 to great success. She soon became one of Australia's most popular poets.

Her political lobbying and writing helped to bring about the 1967 national referendum when over 90% of Australians voted 'Yes' for changes to the laws for the benefit of Aboriginal people. Most voters thought the referendum would bring full citizenship rights to Indigenous Australians but it did not address the issues of equal pay for Aborigines or their personal freedoms. Nevertheless Kath Walker continued her fight for justice and in 1970 she received an **MBE** award medal[1] for her services to Aboriginal people.

As time went by Kath became disappointed by the delay in positive changes and in 1987, just before Australia's Bicentenary, she returned her MBE medal to the government as a protest. Soon after, she changed her name to Oodgeroo Noonuccal to express her Aboriginal heritage.

She decided that education would bring progress faster than politics, so she established an education centre on Stradbroke Island. She said her education program was for 'white kids as well as black. And if there were green ones, I'd like them too ... I'm colour blind, you see. I teach them about Aboriginal culture. I teach them about the balance of nature.'[2]

Her message to the world was: 'The biggest barrier of all between all nations, all class, colour and creed is lack of communication, lack of tolerance, and lack of understanding ... so education is the answer.'[3] Oodgeroo Noonuccal died in 1993, but the messages of her poetry continue.

A) Oodgeroo Noonuccal - Vocabulary activity

Find and highlight the following words and expressions in the story about Oodgeroo Noonuccal. Write them next to the appropriate meaning. One has been done as an example.

<del>heritage</del>   Bicentenary   racial inequality   domestic work   injustice

civil rights movement   delegation   national census   impact   lobbying

national referendum   citizenship rights   volunteered   creed   tolerance

1. _____heritage_____ - something inherited, something belonging to a person's history or culture

2. _____ - unfairness,

3. _____ - different treatment because of a person's race or skin colour

4. _____ - house cleaning or work as a helper in someone's home

5. _____ - offered to do work or activity without being forced to do it

6. _____ - protests in 1950s to 1960s to bring justice & social change

7. _____ - a group of people chosen to represent others

8. _____ - a count of the population by the government

9. _____ - an important effect or influence

10. _____ - trying to change or influence the decisions of government

11. _____ - a time when citizens are asked to vote on an important issue

12. _____ - legal rights of freedom and protection for members of a nation

13. _____ - a celebration 200 years after an important event, e.g. 1788 → 1988

14. _____ - willingness to accept ideas or beliefs different from your own

15. _____ - a belief or religion   Answers, page 148

Notes for page 100

1. MBE means 'Most Excellent Order of the British Empire',

2. Oodgeroo in an interview with Susan Mitchell: The Matriarchs: Twelve Australian Women Talk about their Lives to Susan Mitchell'.(1987), Ringwood, Victoria: Penguin Australia.

3. Oodgeroo in an interview with Bruce Dickson in 1981, during an exhibition of her art in Brisbane, as part of NAIDOC Week.

MBE medal

B) Oodgeroo Noonuccal - Comprehension activity

Work in a group. One person should read aloud each question below.
Discuss the answer to each question together before you write anything.

1) Who was Oodgeroo Noonuccal?

_____

2) Where and when was she born?

_____

3) What did she do after she left school?

_____

4) What movement did she become involved with as an adult?

_____

5) What happened in the following years?

1962: _____

1967: _____

1970: _____

1987: _____

_____

6) What did she believe would bring progress faster than politics, and so what did she establish?

_____

7) What did she believe caused the biggest barrier between people?

_____

8) What did she believe was the answer to problems facing the world?

_____

Answers: page 148

This image illustrated Oodgeroo's poem
'Aboriginal Charter of Rights' in
her book, 'My People' (pages 36-37)
published by The Jacaranda Press, 1970.

Read the first ten lines of
'Aboriginal Charter of Rights'
on the following page.

The image and poem extract (next page) are reproduced by permission of John Wiley & Sons Australia.

C) Poetry

Poetry uses words to create strong images or feelings. Oodgeroo Noonuccal included words in her poems to draw attention to the struggle of Australian Aborigines to achieve human rights.

Read the first ten lines of Oodgeroo's poem:

'Aboriginal Charter of Rights'

We want hope, not racialism.
Brotherhood, not ostracism,
Black advance, not white ascendance:
Make us equals, not dependants.
We need help, not exploitation,
We want freedom, not frustration;
Not control, but self-reliance,
Independence, not compliance,
Not rebuff, but education,
Self-respect, not resignation.

****

by Oodgeroo Noonuccal, 1962

Decide which words in the poem have a positive or negative meaning. as used in <u>the context of the poem</u>.

Answers: page 148

racialism	hope	brotherhood
ostracism	advance	ascendance	equals
dependants	exploitation	freedom
frustration	control	self-reliance
independence	compliance	rebuff
education	self-respect	resignation

positive meaning	negative meaning

D) Language review – Antonyms: words with an opposite meaning

Antonyms are words with an opposite meaning.
Find words in the story about Oodgeroo (page 94) with an opposite meaning to those below. Write them next to their opposites:

words	opposite meaning		words	opposite meaning
small	_____		negative	_____
last	_____		slower	_____

Adding a prefix to make the opposite meaning:

Answers: page 148

Sometimes we make words with an opposite meaning by adding a prefix.
A prefix is a group of letters added to the <u>beginning</u> of a word to make a different meaning.

For example, we make the opposite of 'welcome' by adding the prefix 'un' to make 'unwelcome'.

Find words in the story about Oodgeroo (page 100) with the opposite meaning to those below <u>by adding or taking away</u> a prefix:

justice _____   unpopular _____

equality _____   intolerance _____

D) Language review continued – opposites

We can make words with an opposite meaning by adding a prefix.

A prefix is a group of letters added to the <u>beginning</u> of a word to make a different word.

For example, we make the opposite of 'balance' by adding the prefix 'im' to make 'imbalance'.

Look at some examples of **adjectives with prefixes** added to make the opposite meaning:

adjective	prefix to form the opposite meaning of 'not'	adjectives with the opposite meaning
popular happy necessary even equal married healthy tidy kind sure fit clean well lucky true educated comfortable fair	add 'un' to the beginning of the word	unpopular unhappy unnecessary
honest obedient satisfied	add 'dis' to the beginning of the word	dishonest
secure correct complete appropriate tolerant	add 'in' to the beginning of the word	insecure
possible polite perfect	add 'im' to the beginning of the word	impossible

Spelling – opposites crossword

Make adjectives with the opposite meaning to the following adjectives by adding the correct prefix. Write the words in the crossword next to the numbers.

1. popular   unpopular ✓
2. happy   unhappy ✓
3. necessary
4. even
5. equal
6. healthy
7. tidy

8. married
9. kind
10. sure
11. fit
12. clean
13. true
14. well

15. lucky
16. appropriate
17. honest
18. obedient
19. polite
20. educated
21. fair

22. satisfied
23. possible
24. secure
25. perfect
26. complete
27. correct
28. tolerant

Answers: page 149

Eddie Mabo

Eddie Mabo was a spokesperson for Aboriginal land rights. He believed that Australian laws about land ownership were not right, so he worked hard to get the laws changed.

Photo reproduced with permission of Fairfax photos

Edward Mabo was born on Murray Island, in the Torres Strait, between Australia and New Guinea, in 1936. When he was a baby his mother died, so he lived with his uncle's family. His family had lived on the islands of Torres Strait for many centuries.

In 1879, the government had decided that Murray Island would become part of Australia and would be under the control of the Queensland government. This meant that the indigenous people who lived on the island had no legal power over what happened on the island. However, the Murray Islanders continued to live in their communities and kept up their traditions, customs and beliefs. As part of their lifestyle, they understood the boundaries of their family's land; they understood that particular trees or rocks marked certain boundaries. Their ideas and beliefs about all this were passed on from parents to children, through each generation. And in this way, Eddie Mabo learnt about his land and culture.

When he was seventeen, he left Murray Island to live in Queensland. He had different jobs and wherever he worked, he became a spokesperson for the other Aboriginal workers. When he was twenty-three he met and married Bonita and they had ten children. In 1974, he became a gardener at a university and that year was a turning point for Eddie Mabo. He wanted to improve his education, so he attended seminars at the university and read library books about his people and their traditions. He talked with the professors at the university about his culture and he proudly told them about his family's land on Murray Island. They tried to explain that all the land on Murray Island belonged to the government so his family couldn't own any land there. He was shocked and said, 'No way, it's not theirs, it's ours.' Then he learnt about the laws that said Aboriginal people who had lived on Murray Island for centuries, had no legal right to their land and no legal power over what happened on the island.

Mabo decided he must do something to change the laws that he believed were so wrong. First, he had to learn more about the situation so he could find the best way to change it. Through study, he learnt that after the British found and claimed the land of Australia in 1770, they'd said it was 'terra nullius', meaning 'no-one's land'. Mabo decided to challenge that idea. At a Land Rights Conference in 1981, Mabo made an important speech. He explained clearly how land was given from parents to their children on Murray Island. He said that the land had been stolen from his people when the government decided to take it as theirs. He said he was the rightful owner of the land owned by his father's family. He believed he could win the fight for his land without violence.

Court battles continued for more than ten years but Eddie remained confident. In 1992, when he knew he was dying of cancer, he continued to believe his people would get justice through the High Court of Australia. Five months after his death, the court announced the historic decision that it was wrong to say the land was 'terra nullius' when the British arrived two hundred years earlier. Mabo's case showed that Aboriginal and Islander people could prove their right to the land they had lived on for centuries. Eddie Mabo had won a victory with education rather than violence, and had changed the course of Australia's history!

A) Eddie Mabo - Vocabulary activity

Find and highlight the following words and expressions in the story about Edward Mabo.
Write them next to their appropriate meaning. The first one has been done as an example.

ownership	~~spokesperson~~ ✓	indigenous	centuries	traditions	no legal power
generation	boundaries	a turning point	to challenge	seminars	proudly
claimed	no legal right	court battles	without violence	justice	won a victory

1) __spokesperson__ – someone who represents and speaks for a group of people

2) _____ - owning something; it belongs to you by law

3) _____ - hundreds of years

4) _____ - describing the people and animals that have always lived in a place

5) _____ - not allowed to have control; not allowed to make laws or change laws

6) _____ - customs; ways of doing things by a group of people for a long time

7) _____ - borders or lines that divide two areas of land

8) _____ - period of time from birth to the age of becoming a parent, about 25 years

9) _____ - a time when an important change begins in someone's life

10) _____ - discussion classes at university

11) _____ - happily, in a way that shows you are very pleased about something

12) _____ - not allowed by law to have something or do something

13) _____ - stated or said something belongs to you; that it's your property

14) _____ - to say you don't agree with an idea, law or decision

15) _____ - when nobody gets hurt or killed

16) _____ - disagreements or arguments between groups of people in a law court

17) _____ - have good and fair treatment; fairness

18) _____ - showed that you were successful in a fight or competition

Answers: page 150

B) Eddie Mabo - Comprehension activity

Discuss the answer to each question before writing anything.   Answers: page 150

1) Who was Eddie Mabo?

_____

2) Where was he born and how long had his family lived there?

_____

3) What did the government decide about Murray Island in 1879?

_____

4) What did the government's decision mean for the people who lived on Murray Island?

_____

5) What did he talk about with the professors at the university?

_____

6) What did the professors explain to Eddie about the land on Murray Island?

_____

7) What did Eddie decide to do when he heard that the government owned Murray Island?

_____

8) What does the expression 'terra nullius' mean?

_____

9) What did Eddie Mabo explain in his speech in 1981?

_____

10) What did the court announce after his death and what did his court case show?

_____

11) How did Eddie Mabo win his victory?

_____

Map activity

Check an atlas and mark the approximate
location of Murray Island on the map.

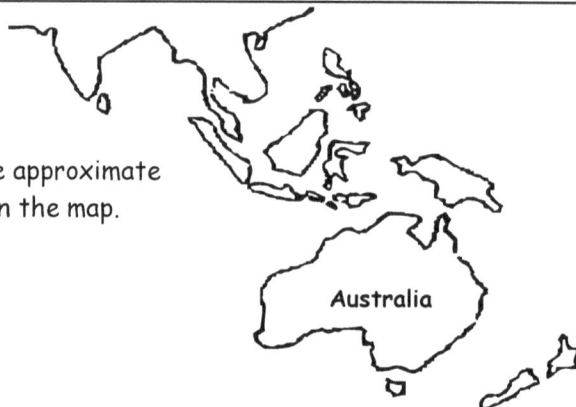

Australia

C) Language activities - Words and phrases that show 'ownership'

In English, we can show 'ownership' or 'who something belongs to' by one of the following ways:

1) Add <u>apostrophe + s</u>: For example: It is **David's car**. (The car belongs to David.)

2) Use the preposition '<u>of</u>' to show who or what something belongs to.
    For example: It is a **law** <u>of</u> **Australia**. (meaning 'the law belongs to Australia')

3) Use a word such as *my, his, her, your, our, their* <u>before a noun</u> to show ownership.
    For example: It is **his** car. (The car belongs to him.)

4) Use a possessive pronoun such as: *mine, his, hers, ours, yours* or *theirs* <u>after a noun</u>.
    For example: The idea was **theirs**. (The idea belongs to them.)

Possessive pronouns			
Look at the following table with examples of possessive pronouns:			
single possessive pronouns		plural possessive pronouns	
examples:		examples:	
mine	Is that book mine?	**ours**	Is that book ours?
yours	Is that book yours?	**yours**	Is that book yours?
his	The book is his.	} **theirs**	No, the book is theirs.
hers	The book is hers.		

Practice 1: Highlight words and phrases in the following sentences about Eddie Mabo that show 'ownership' of something. One has been done as an example.

1) Edward Mabo was born on Murray Island, in 1936. When he was a baby his mother died, so he lived with his uncle's family.

2) His family had lived on the islands of Torres Strait for many centuries.

3) He wanted to improve his education, so he attended seminars at the university and read library books about his people and their traditions.

4) He talked with the professors at the university about his culture and he proudly told them about his family's land on Murray Island.

Practice 2: Complete the following sentences from Eddie Mabo's story (page 106) with words or phrases that show 'ownership'.

5) He was shocked and said, 'No way, it's not_____, it's _____.' (Line 25)

6) He said the land had been stolen from his people when the government decided to take it as _____. (Line 33)

7) He said he was the rightful owner of the land owned by _____ family. He believed he could win the fight for_____ land without violence. (Line 34)

8) Eddie had won a victory with education rather than violence and changed the course _____

_____. (Line 41)

Answers: page 150

Charles Perkins

Charles Perkins was an Aboriginal activist who spent his life fighting racism and discrimination. He was the first Aboriginal Australian to complete a university degree. He was also well known for his soccer skills.

Charles Perkins was born in 1936, in Alice Springs in Central Australia. When he was ten years old he was sent to school in Adelaide far away from his family. After he left school, he played soccer professionally and went to England for two years to play for different soccer teams.

While he was away from his country he realised that discrimination was holding back his people in Australia. When he returned to Australia, he joined the Federal Council for the Advancement of Aborigines. He wanted to confront white Australians about their treatment of Aboriginal people.

In 1963, Charles became one of the first Aboriginal students at the University of Sydney. While he was at university, he met white students who agreed that something should be done about discrimination against Aboriginal people. These students knew about the 'Freedom Rides' in America, where students travelled around in buses to protest about racism against black Americans. They decided to do the same thing in Australia.

In 1965, with about thirty other students, Charles Perkins organised a bus to travel to towns in outback Australia. It became known as the 'Freedom Ride'. The students wanted to get the facts about racism against Aborigines in country towns and to increase public awareness about what was happening to Aboriginal people. For example, in one town the local council had banned Aborigines from using the public swimming pool. In other places, Aboriginal people were not allowed to go into clubs or cinemas. The students of the 'Freedom Ride' stood for many hours outside these places, protesting against what was happening. Many white people in the country towns were hostile to the students because they didn't want publicity. However, the stories reached national and international media. This raised awareness about what was happening and helped to bring changes to discrimination laws.

In 1966 Charles Perkins graduated from the University of Sydney as the first Aboriginal Australian with a university degree. From 1969 he began work as a researcher in the Office of Aboriginal Affairs. Research then showed that less than 10% of Aboriginal children finished high school. Charles had a burning passion for advancing the interests of his people and worked hard to improve government policies.

As he got older, Charles developed kidney disease and by 1972 he needed to have a kidney transplant. But he continued to work hard for 'a fair go' for Aboriginal Australians. In 1981 he became the head of the Commonwealth Department of Aboriginal Affairs and in 1987 he was made an 'Officer of the Order of Australia'.

Sadly, in the year 2000 he died due to kidney problems. He was the longest living kidney transplant patient to that time. During his final years Charles put his energy into Aboriginal youth education. After he died, newspapers wrote that 'Australia had lost a true champion'.
The Charlie Perkins Children's Trust was formed in 2002 in his memory.

A) Charles Perkins - Vocabulary activity

Find the following words and expressions in the story about Charles Perkins and write them next to the appropriate meaning. The first one has been done as an example.

racism	~~activist~~ ✓	confront	discrimination	protest	banned
public awareness		hostile	a burning passion	government policies	
champion		a fair go	kidney transplant	youth	

1. _____activist_____ - someone who tries to make social or political changes

2. _____ - a belief that people of another race aren't as good as your own race

3. _____ - the bad treatment of someone due to their race, religion, age or sex

4. _____ - talk about a difficult situation with the people responsible for it

5. _____ - to say that you disagree with something that is happening

6. _____ - when people are told and know about something that is happening in society

7. _____ - when something is not allowed

8. _____ - acting in an angry way

9. _____ - a very strong belief and feeling about something

10. _____ - a government's ideas, plans and way of acting about particular issues

11. _____ - an operation in which another person's kidney is put into someone's body

12. _____ - a fair, honest and equal way to treat all people

13. _____ - young people

14. _____ - someone who fights for better conditions and someone to be proud of

Answers: page 151

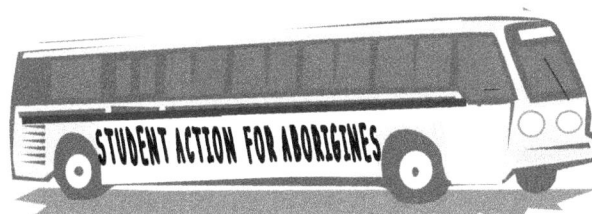

The 'Freedom Ride' bus of 1965

B) Charles Perkins - Comprehension activity

Work in a group. One person should read aloud each question below.
Discuss the answer to each question together before you write anything.

1) Who was Charles Perkins?

_____

2) When and where was he born?

_____

3) What did Charles Perkins do when he left school?

_____

4) What did he realise while he was away from Australia?

_____

5) What happened in 1963?

_____

6) What did he do in 1965?

_____

7) Why did Charles organise the Freedom Ride with other students?

_____

8) What was the result of the 'Freedom Ride'?

_____

9) What happened in the following years?

1966: _____

1969: _____

1972: _____

1981: _____

1987: _____

10) How was he described in 2000 and what organisation was formed in his name?

_____

_____

Answers: page 151

C) Language activities - more about verbs: infinitives

It is common in English for one verb to follow directly after another verb. For example, this happens when we talk about our intention or attitude to an action. For example: He **wanted to play** soccer.

The **first verb** refers to the **intention**. The **second verb** refers to the **action**.

He **wanted**	**to play** soccer.

Look at some more examples:

The **first verb** refers to the **attitude or intention**. The **second verb** refers to the **action**.

He **wanted**	**to study** at university.
He **decided**	**to help** the students.
He **began**	**to protest** about racism.

In the sentences above, the second verb is called an **infinitive**, eg. to study, to help, to protest.

Only **some** English verbs can be followed by an infinitive.
Read the list of some verbs that can be followed by infinitives.

Underline the <u>verb followed by an infinitive</u> in the sentences below. Answers, page 151.

like	-	She <u>likes to start</u> work early.
hope	-	They hope to buy a house soon.
want	-	Tom wants to study French next year.
learn	-	You must learn to spell correctly.
decide	-	We decided to leave early.
plan	-	We plan to go overseas next year.
promise	-	He promised to take me to the movie.
try	-	I'll try to finish the job by 5 o'clock.
offer	-	He offered to help us finish the work..
begin	-	Mary began to cry.
continue	-	David continued to study.
forget	-	He forgot to save the document.
remember	-	Remember to go left at the corner.
refuse	-	He refused to stop.
help	-	They helped to repair the car.
go	-	I'll go to see him tomorrow.

Note:
Some verbs can be followed by an **infinitive** or a verb with **'ing'** to make the same meaning.

For example: 'She **began to cry**.' means the same as:
          'She **began crying**.'

Always check a grammar book if you're not sure about the correct way to use English verbs.

Practice: Complete the following sentences about Charles Perkins with a verb followed by an infinitive. You can find the answers by checking the story on page 110, or see answers page 152.

1) He _____ white Australians about their treatment of Aboriginal people. (line 12)

2) They _____ the same thing in Australia. (line 17)

3) The students _____ the facts about racism against Aborigines in country towns. (line 19)

4) Aboriginal people were _____ into clubs or cinemas. (line 22)

5) By 1972 he _____ a kidney transplant. (line 34)

6) He _____ hard for 'a fair go' for Aboriginal Australians. (line 35)

Revision - prepositions

Prepositions show the relationship between words in a sentence. See examples on pages 35 and 73.
Use the prepositions in the box below to complete sentences about Charles Perkins.
You can use the prepositions in the box more than once.   Answers: page 152

about	as	for	from	in	into	of

1) He was well known _____ his soccer skills.

2) After he left school, he played soccer professionally and went to England _____ two years to play _____ different soccer teams.

3) While he was away _____ his country he realised that discrimination was holding back his people _____ Australia.

4) He wanted to confront white Australians _____ their treatment of Aboriginal people.

5) He met white students who agreed that something should be done _____ discrimination against Aboriginal people.

6) These students knew _____ the 'Freedom Rides' in America, where students travelled around _____ buses to protest _____ racism against black Americans.

7) In one town the local council had banned Aborigines _____ using the public swimming pool.

8) In other places Aboriginal people could not go _____ clubs or cinemas.

9) From 1969 he began work _____ a researcher _____ the Office of Aboriginal Affairs.

10) Research then showed that less than 10% _____ Aboriginal children finished high school.

11) During his final years Charlie his put his energy _____ Aboriginal youth education.

Guide to pronunciation of the letter 'c'

The letter 'c' can be pronounced in three different ways.

In dictionaries, pronunciation of a word is generally shown between diagonal lines / / eg. central /sentəl/

1) The letter 'c' is usually pronounced as the sound /s/ when followed by the letters 'i', 'e' or'y',
   For example, the pronunciation of 'cell' is /sel/. The pronunciation of 'cent' is /sent/.

2) The letter 'c ' is pronounced as the sound /k/ when followed by any other letter.

   As an example, look at the word council. The first 'c' is pronounced as the sound /k/;
   the second 'c' is pronounced as the sound /s/ because it is followed by the letter 'i'.

3) The letters 'ch' together have a special pronunciation, as in Charles, children, champion
   (an exception is the word 'school' in which the letter 'h ' is silent).

Practice - pronunciation of the letter 'c'

Using the spelling guide on page 114 put the words below in the correct column to show how the letter 'c' is pronounced?

~~club~~   ~~office~~   racism   central   places   cinemas
decided   activist   country   century   public   publicity
once   office   December   peace

letter 'c' pronounced as the sound /s/	letter 'c' pronounced as the sound /k/
office	club

Crossword – spelling practice

Write the meanings to the following clues using words with the letter 'c', pronounced as the sound /s/.
Write the words in the crossword next to the numbers. One has been done as an example.
Note: The answer words are in the story about Charles Perkins (page 110) on the line number below.

1) a very large town _____city_____

2) belief that people of another race aren't as good as your own race _____ (line 2)

3) in the middle _____ (line 6)

4) the progress of something _____ (line 11)

5) made a decision, chose to do something (past tense) _____ (line 17)

6) local government, the group of people who control a local area _____ (line 21)

7) buildings where you go to watch movies _____ (line 23)

8) areas _____ (line 23)

9) advertising so that people get information about something _____ (line 25)

10) a room or building where an organisation works _____ (line 29)

11) government's plans or ways of acting about particular issues _____ (line 32)

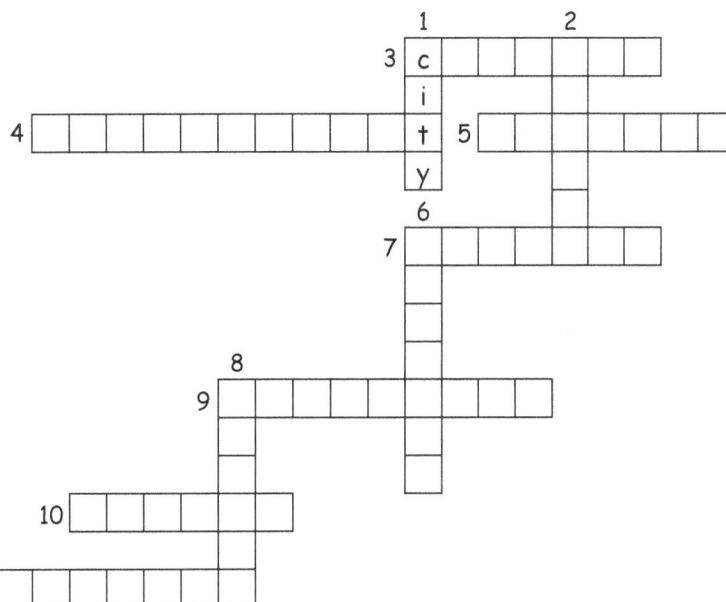

Answers: page 152

People in Australia's Past   115   www.boyereducation.com.au

Group Activities
People in Australia's Past Quiz

Take turns answering the questions. The map on page 117 will help explain some answers.

1) How did the **Aboriginal people** live on the Australian continent in a sustainable way?

2) Where did **Arthur Phillip** establish the first European settlement in Australia?

3) Where is **Bennelong** Point? How did it get that name?

4) Why was **James Ruse's** land called 'Experiment Farm'?

5) Where did **Mary Reibey** establish her business? Why is she famous?

6) What did **John** and **Elizabeth Macarthur** establish on 'Elizabeth Farm'?

7) Where did **Governor Macquarie** establish the first inland city?

8) Why did **Caroline Chisholm** establish the 'Female Immigrants' Home'?

9) What were the names of the six colonies of Australia when **Edmund Barton** became Australia's Prime Minister in 1901? How has the map of Australia changed since then?

10) Where did **Edith Cowan** live as a young woman? Why is she famous?

11) Where did **'Banjo' Paterson** live as a young boy? What famous song did he write?

12) Where was **Nellie Melba** born? Why is she famous?

13) Where did **David Unaipon** write about in his first publication? What did he invent?

14) Where did **Charles Kingsford Smith** fly on his first non-stop flight across Australia?

15) In which states of Australia did **John Flynn** first travel and see the problems of isolated communities in the Australian outback? What did he do as a result?

16) Where did **Douglas Mawson** work before going to Antarctica? What did he accomplish?

17) Where was **Vincent Lingiari** born and what happened there?

18) Where was **Oodgeroo Noonuccal** born and what did she later establish there?

19) Where was **Eddie Mabo** born? Why is he famous?

20) Where was **Charles Perkins** born? What did he do while he was a university student?

Answers to all questions are found in the stories of **'People in Australia's Past'**.
Find the answers by checking the story of the people named in each question.

Make your own list of questions about people in Australia's past for other people to answer.

Map activity

Use the map of Australia to discuss where people lived and where things happened in the stories about 'People in Australia's Past'.

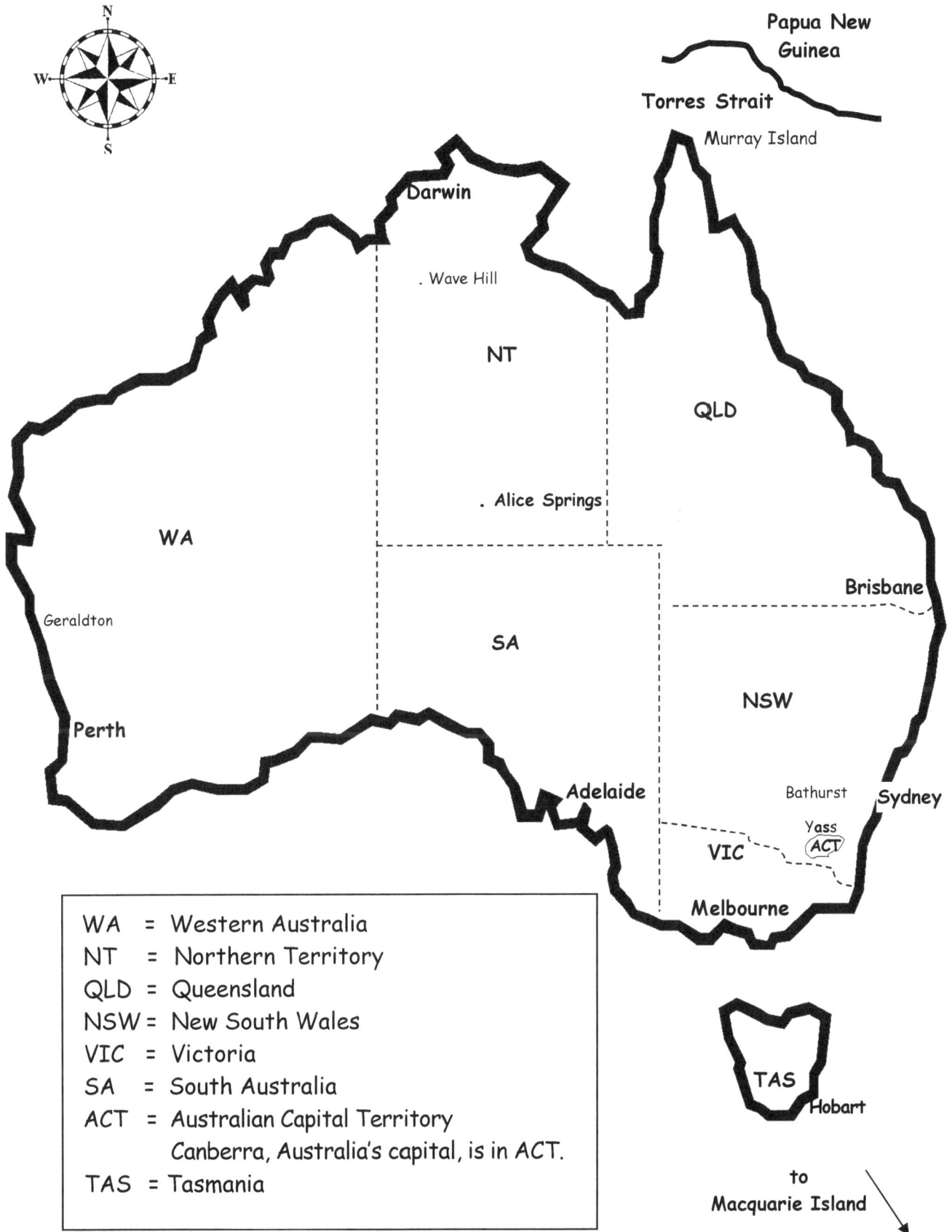

N
W **E**
S

Papua New Guinea

Torres Strait

Murray Island

Darwin

. Wave Hill

NT

QLD

. Alice Springs

WA

Geraldton

SA

Brisbane

NSW

Perth

Adelaide

Bathurst   **Sydney**

Yass
ACT

VIC

Melbourne

WA	= Western Australia
NT	= Northern Territory
QLD	= Queensland
NSW	= New South Wales
VIC	= Victoria
SA	= South Australia
ACT	= Australian Capital Territory
	Canberra, Australia's capital, is in ACT.
TAS	= Tasmania

TAS

Hobart

to Macquarie Island

Note:
This map shows approximate locations; for more precise positions of cities, towns and borders, check an atlas.

Information exchange about people in Australia's past

In the following activity, students read a story about a person in Australia's past (from this book or another source) and complete the summary table on page 119. Then they exchange their information with another person or group who has read and summarised a story about a different person in Australia's past.

* Page 119 provides space for exchanging information about two people; page 120 provides space for exchanging information about three people in Australia's past for further practice.

Exchanging information about people in Australia's past: Instructions
Step 1

Complete the first column of the summary table by answering the four questions with information about a person from Australia's past. Write <u>simple</u> answers that can be explained easily to other people.

Step 2

Work with another person, exchanging information by asking each other the questions.

When you tell your partner about the person you have researched, explain your information simply. Don't just read the answers; use your own words to share the information.

Step 3

Ask your partner the questions listed on the 'People in Australia's past' summary table. <u>Don't copy their written answers</u> as this activity is for listening and speaking practice.

Sample of a completed summary table

People in Australia's past

What is the famous person's name?	Dame Nellie Melba	David Unaipon
Why is the person famous?	She was a famous singer.	He was an inventor and writer.
What other interesting or important things did the person do?	She was Australia's first superstar and the first musician to do radio broadcasts.	He was the first Aboriginal Australian to write published books.
What award or recognition has the person received?	She was made a Dame of the British Empire. Her picture is on Australia's $100 note.	The 'David Unaipon award' honours his work. His picture is on Australia's $50 note.

People in Australia's past – summary table

Complete the first column in the summary table below with simple information about a famous person in Australia's past.

Listen: Ask another person questions to learn the main points about a famous person in Australia's past. Write short answers below.

Speak: Tell another person about the famous person. Explain the story in your own words (don't read the information).

What is the famous person's name?		
Why is the person famous?		
What other interesting or important things did the person do?		
What award or recognition has the person received?		

Self assessment

Did you get the information you needed? yes ☐ no ☐

Did you check information and ask for repetition if you didn't understand? yes ☐ no ☐

Did you show successful listening skills in this activity? yes ☐ no ☐

Did you show successful speaking skills in this activity? yes ☐ no ☐

People in Australia's past – summary table

Complete the first column in the summary table below with simple information about a famous person in Australia's past.

Speak: Tell two other people about the famous person. Explain the story in your own words (don't read the information).

Listen: Ask two people questions to learn the main points about two other famous people in Australia's past. Write short answers below.

What is the famous person's name?		
Why is the person famous?		
What other interesting or important things did the person do?		
What award or recognition has the person received?		

Self assessment

Did you get the information you needed?   yes ☐   no ☐

Did you check information and ask for repetition if you didn't understand?   yes ☐   no ☐

Did you show successful listening skills in this activity?   yes ☐   no ☐

Did you show successful speaking skills in this activity?   yes ☐   no ☐

Writing a simple biography

A biography is a recount of someone's life story. A recount often has the following structure.

Title: Who is the story about?

Setting: Who? When and where did events happen? This is covered in one or two paragraphs.

Events: Tell what happened in the order that things happened.
Start a new paragraph for each major event.

Ending: Tell how the story ends. As an optional addition, the writer
can add a comment about how the person is remembered.

> Use this model to
> write a biography of
> a famous Australian .

Title:

Setting:
Who?
Where?
When?
Why?

Events:
What
happened?

Ending:
and
optional
comment

Answers

A) Australian Aborigines - Vocabulary activity

1) _____residents_____ – people who live in a particular place
2) _____continent_____ – a main area of land on the earth, such as Africa, Asia, America, Australia
3) _____sustainable_____ - in ways that do not harm the environment but consider future needs
4) _____tribes_____ - societies or family groups who share a community, culture and way of life
5) _____settlers_____ - a group of people who move to a new place to live there
6) _____respected_____ - believed to be important and something to be cared for
7) _____camps_____ - places where people stay for a short time (sometimes in tents)
8) _____possessions_____ - things that are owned by people, things that belong to people
9) _____gathering_____ - collecting food and things that are needed
10) _____thieves_____ - people who steal things from other people
11) _____revenge_____ - hurt or harms someone because they had hurt someone you know
12) _clash of cultures_ - fight or disagree because ideas or cultures are different
13) _bush survival skills_ - skills that make it easy to live in the Australian bush
14) _effective_ - successful, does a job very well
15) _compass_ - something that shows which direction to go
16) _superior_ - (someone who thinks they are) better or in a higher position than other people

B) Australian Aborigines – Comprehension activity

1. The first residents in Australia were the Aboriginal people.
2. Aborigines taught their children about their history and culture through paintings on rocks and through dance, songs and stories called Dreamtime stories.
3. The stories explained how the world began. They told the people how they must behave, how to find food and how to care for the land.
4. They believed they were part of nature, so they respected it and used only what they needed. They found enough food by moving between camps at different times of the year.
5. Europeans cut down trees, put up fences, built towns, collected possessions and believed that it was important to own the land.
6. When the British arrived in Australia, they decided the land wasn't owned by anyone because they saw no cities, fences or roads.
7. Many of the Aborigines were helpful to the settlers until they saw the settlers were making farms where Aboriginal hunting and gathering places had always been.
8. They knew how to find water in dry places. They could start a fire by rubbing sticks together. They had tools and weapons that were simple but very effective. They moved from place to place without a compass or maps.
9. Answers to the problems of today's world, such as how to protect our natural environment and how to live in a sustainable way, were known and practised by Aborigines thousands of years ago.

C) Language activities - verbs

Past tense	Present tense
lived	live
moved	move
arrived	arrive
believed	believe
needed	need
tried	try

Past tense	Present tense
was	is
knew	know
thought	think
told	tell
were	are
had	have

Past tense verbs – crossword

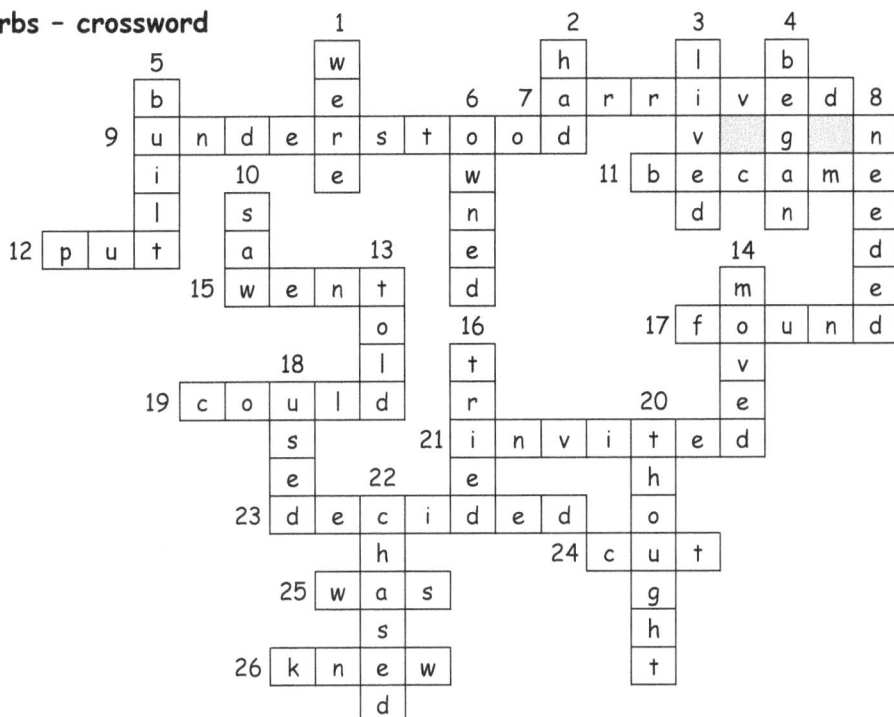

```
                                1              2       3      4
              5                 w              h       l      b
              b                6  7  a  r  r  i  v  e  d  8
         9  u  n  d  e  r  s  t  o  o  d        v     g     n
         i        10  e              w     11 b  e  c  a  m  e
         l         s              w           d        n     e
12 p  u  t        a           13              14             d
         15 w  e  n  t           d              m           e
                    o        16              17 f  o  u  n  d
              18    l        t                v
         19 c  o  u  l  d              20     e
              s           21 i  n  v  i  t  e  d
              e  22        e                 h
         23 d  e  c  i  d  e  d              o
              h              24 c  u  t     g
         25 w  a  s                          h
              s                              t
         26 k  n  e  w
              d
```

Aboriginal Australians: Put verbs in the correct places in the story about Aboriginal Australians

Aborigines lived in Australia for thousands of years before people arrived from Europe. They taught their children about their culture through paintings on rocks and through dance, songs and stories. Each story had a special message about the laws of the tribe and information about how to find food and how to care for the land.

Aborigines lived in a sustainable way. They found enough food by moving between camps at different times of the year. Because they moved from place to place they didn't have many possessions. These things about Aboriginal culture were different from European culture. Europeans cut down trees, put up fences, built towns and believed that it was important to own the land.

When the British arrived in Australia, they decided the land wasn't owned by anyone because they saw no cities, fences or roads. At first, meetings between the British and Aboriginal people were careful but friendly. Many Aborigines were helpful to the settlers until they saw the settlers were making farms where Aboriginal hunting and gathering places had always been. Soon there was not enough food left for them and they became hungry. However, when Aborigines went to the farms to pick the food growing there, they were chased away as thieves and many were killed. The Aboriginal people then killed white people in revenge and a clash of cultures began.

Aborigines had bush survival skills that the Europeans didn't know or understand. They knew how to find water in dry places and they could start a fire by rubbing sticks together. They had tools and weapons that were simple but very effective. They moved from place to place to gather their food without compass or maps. Many of the Europeans thought they were superior to the black people and never tried to learn from them. As a result, many white people died when they got lost in the Australian bush.

A) Arthur Phillip - Vocabulary activity

1) __settlement__ - a new place or town built by people after arriving from another place
2) __governor__ - a person who governs a place that is controlled by another country
3) __colony__ - a place that is ruled and controlled by a far-away country
4) __fleet__ - a group of ships traveling together
5) __convicts__ - prisoners, people put in prison for doing bad things
6) __authority__ - the power to make decisions and control other people
7) __voyage__ - a long trip to another place by ship
8) __harbour__ - an area of water next to land where ships can be left safely
9) __challenges__ - difficult situations; things that test people's ability
10) __landed__ - went on to the land after being on the water (sea, river or lake)
11) __food shortage__ - not enough food for people
12) __equipment__ - tools or things needed and used to do a job
13) __inadequate__ - not good enough for the job or situation, not adequate
14) __an optimist__ - a positive person, someone who believes the best things are possible
15) __imagine__ - to think about something, to have a picture or idea in your mind

B) Comprehension - activity

1) Arthur Phillip was the leader of the first British settlement in Australia. He was the first governor of the colony of New South Wales.
2) When he was 48, he was chosen as leader of a fleet of eleven ships that would take hundreds of convicts to a place on the other side of the world.
3) He was chosen for the job because he had experience in sailing, farming and in leading men.
4) He had to take enough food for the long voyage and for the first year in the new place because they didn't know what food grew there.
5) The voyage of 12,000 miles had taken eight months and one week.
6) Arthur Phillip found a place for the new settlement beside a good harbour. This place is now the world famous Sydney Harbour.
7) There were more than a thousand people on the ships and more than 700 of them were convicts.
8) When they landed, it was during the heat of summer.
   There were no houses or buildings to protect them from the hot or wet weather.
   There were no fields planted with vegetables or fruit.
   Many of the convicts were sick or weak from being on a ship for so long. Some had died on the voyage.
   Most of them came from cities and knew nothing about farming or building.
   The ground around the settlement was too hard and dry to grow enough food and their equipment and tools were inadequate.
9) He decided the best idea was to get the convicts to work by offering them more freedom and the chance to farm their own piece of land if they behaved well.
10) Arthur Phillip laid the foundation for the nation of Australia.

C) Language activities - Grouping ideas together in writing

The main idea of paragraph 1 is:	c) who Arthur Phillip was
The main idea of paragraph 2 is:	b) Arthur Phillip's early life and career
The main idea of paragraph 3 is:	b) Phillip was chosen to be leader of the first fleet
The main idea of paragraph 4 is:	b) planning for the voyage
The main idea of paragraph 5 is:	a) the voyage
The main idea of paragraph 6 is:	a) the challenges of the new settlement
The main idea of paragraph 7 is:	a) Phillip's ideas for the convicts
The main idea of paragraph 8 is:	a) the result of Arthur Phillip's work

Nouns - Equipment brought to Australia on the First Fleet of 1788.

1. candles
2. fish hooks
3. rope
4. hammer and nails
5. tents
6. hammock
7. hatchet
8. handsaw
9. hinges
10. carriage
11. padlocks
12. pickaxe
13. cotton thread
14. shovel
15. cooking pot
16. axe
17. cart
18. handcuffs
19. hoe
20. wheelbarrow

Crossword - Equipment

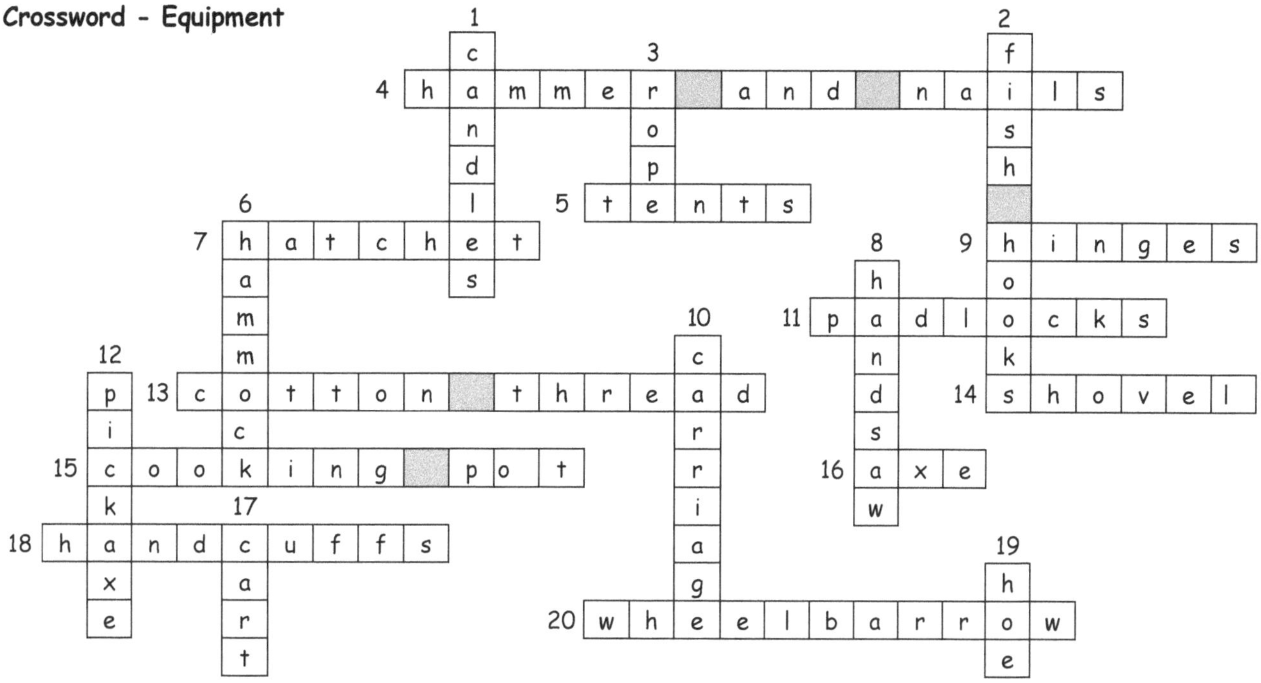

(Crossword grid with answers filled in)

1. candle
2. fish
3. rope
4. hammer and nails
5. tents
6. hammock
7. hatchet
8. hand
9. hinges
10. carriage
11. padlocks
12. pickaxe
13. cotton thread
14. shovel
15. cooking pot
16. axe
17. cart
18. handcuffs
19. hoe
20. wheelbarrow

Joining ideas or different pieces of information in sentences

1) He joined the British Navy <u>when</u> he was sixteen years old.

2) <u>While</u> he was not sailing with the navy, he lived on his farm in England.

3) He was chosen for the job <u>because</u> he had experience sailing, farming and in leading men.

4) When they landed, it was during the heat of summer <u>but</u> there were no houses <u>or</u> buildings to protect them from the hot weather.

5) There was a great food shortage <u>so</u> everyone, including Governor Phillip, had very little food.

6) <u>Although</u> there were many problems, Governor Phillip was an optimist!

7) They were on an island <u>so</u> it would be difficult to leave.

8) He decided the best idea was to get the convicts to work by offering them more freedom <u>and</u> the chance to farm their own piece of land <u>if</u> they behaved well.

9) He imagined what was possible <u>if</u> people worked hard and worked together.

Map Activity

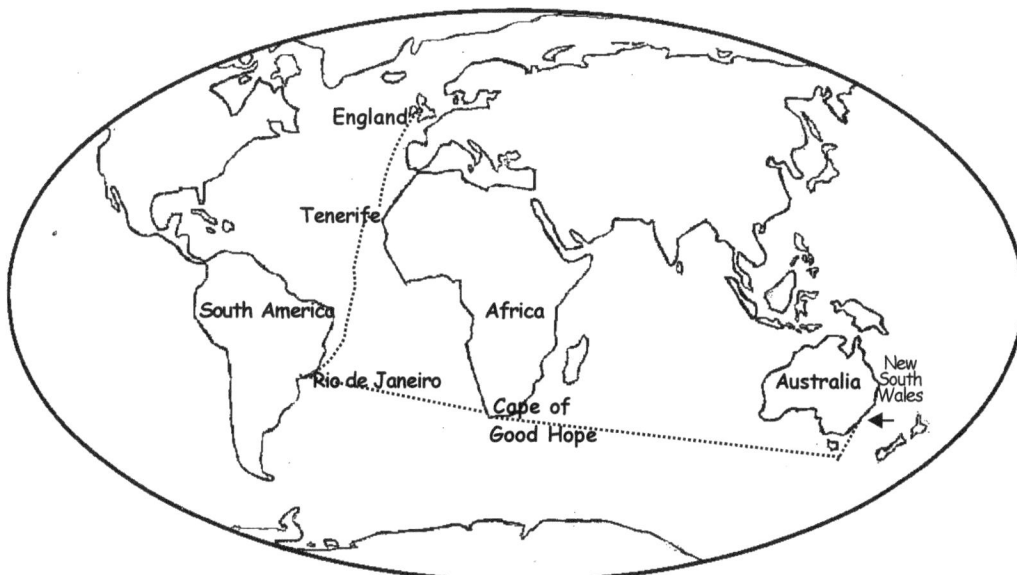

A) Bennelong – Vocabulary activity

1. __mediator__ - a person who helps to make peace between two groups of people
2. __shocked__ - had a sudden bad feeling because of something seen or heard
3. __taking over__ - start using and controlling something that belongs to other people
4. __beaten__ - being hit many times by another person
5. __in chains__ - metal pieces around the legs to stop a prisoner from running
6. __kidnap__ - take someone away from their home and keep them as a prisoner
7. __grabbed__ - to be caught and taken hold of by someone suddenly
8. __eventually__ - after some time has gone by
9. __made jokes__ - told funny stories to make people laugh
10. __escaped__ - left or got away from a place or situation that he didn't like
11. __climate__ - the weather conditions
12. __homesick__ - feeling sad because you are away from your home and family
13. __depressed__ - a feeling of being very unhappy
14. __intelligent__ - clever
15. __good-humoured__ - happy and friendly
16. __open-minded__ - happy to listen to ideas or opinions that are new and different to yours
17. __diplomats__ - people who keep good and peaceful relations between two nations

B) Bennelong - Comprehension activity

1) Bennelong was **a mediator between Aboriginal and European cultures.**
2) The Aborigines didn't like the British cutting down trees, taking over their hunting and fishing places and building houses and fences. They were shocked to see convicts being beaten by soldiers and working in chains.
3) Bennelong was grabbed on a beach and taken to Governor Phillip's house as a prisoner.
4) He saw that he was being treated well and eventually a friendship began between him and Governor Phillip. He began calling the Governor by an Aboriginal word which meant 'father' and Phillip called Bennelong by an Aboriginal name meaning 'son'. Bennelong lived and ate well in the Governor's house. He learnt English and wore European clothes. He drank wine and made jokes with the officers.
5) He was not free to leave whenever he wished and he missed his freedom and his own cultural ways.
6) Governor Phillip promised Bennelong that if he returned to the Sydney settlement, he would have complete freedom to return to his people whenever he wished.
7) When Governor Phillip returned to England in 1792, Bennelong decided to go with him.
8) Bennelong had problems living in the cold English climate and became very homesick. He began drinking too much alcohol and became sick and depressed
9) Bennelong was an intelligent, good-humoured and open-minded man, who tried to improve the relationship between his culture and one that was very different to his.
10) He is remembered today as one of Australia's first diplomats.

C) Language activities - Nouns

People	Places	Nationalities
Bennelong	England	European
Governor Phillip	Sydney	British

Concrete nouns			Abstract nouns
places	people	things	conditions, experiences and feelings
beach	mediator son	trees	culture climate
settlement	settlers father	houses	friendship health
harbour	convicts man	fences	time
	prisoner officers	chains	freedom
	diplomat	clothes	problems

A) James Ruse – Vocabulary activity

1) _____pioneer_____ – the first person to do something and then show other people the way
2) _self-sufficient_ - having everything necessary to live, to be independent
3) _____arrested_____ - caught and asked questions by police about a crime, maybe put in prison
4) _____punishment_____ - when a person is made to suffer because they did something bad
5) _____colony_____ - a place that is ruled and controlled by a far-away country
6) _____First Fleet_____ - the first group of 11 ships to arrive in Sydney with convicts
7) _____starve_____ - die from hunger, not have enough food to keep living
8) _____seasons_____ - parts of the year: summer, winter, autumn, spring
9) _____unfamiliar_____ - different, not understood or not known before
10) _____give it a go_____ - try to do something
11) _____well-behaved_____ - being good and doing the right thing
12) _____experiment_____ - a test to see if something is possible and to see if it will succeed
13) _____survive_____ - continue to live through a difficult situation
14) _____methods_____ - ways of doing something
15) _____land grant_____ - land given to someone by the government
16) _____droughts_____ - long periods of time without rain, when there is not enough water

B) James Ruse – Comprehension activity

1) James Ruse was a pioneer farmer. He was the first of Australia's convicts to be given land for farming.
2) When he was 23 years old he was arrested for stealing two silver watches.
3) He was sent as a convict to work for seven years in the colony in Sydney, New South Wales.
4) Governor Phillip knew they must grow their own food or they would starve.
   The land around Sydney was hard and not good for growing vegetables.
   Some of the convicts were sick and weak. Many were lazy and not interested in trying to grow anything.
   The weather was very hot and so many things were new and unfamiliar.
5) He wanted to give it a go. He told Governor Phillip he had experience as a farmer. He asked if he could have some land to grow food and show that he could become self-sufficient in a short period of time.
6) Governor Phillip allowed this because he saw that James Ruse was a well-behaved convict. He also wanted to see if it was possible to succeed in farming in a country where the seasons and the soil where unfamiliar.
7) They were given clothes, tools, chickens, vegetable seeds and help to clear and dig more land.
8) Governor Phillip was very pleased because the success of James and his wife made other convicts want to try the same methods. Within a few months, a farming community began near the Parramatta River.
9) As a reward Governor Phillip gave James the title to his farm.
10) They showed that anyone can create their own success, even when other people don't believe it is possible.

C) Language activities - Nouns revision

James Ruse was a pioneer <u>farmer</u> in Australia. He was the first <u>convict</u> in Australia to be given <u>land</u> for farming.

James Ruse was born on a farm in England in 1759. When he was 23, police arrested him for stealing two silver <u>watches</u>. For <u>punishment</u>, he was sent to work for seven <u>years</u> in the <u>colony</u> of New South Wales. He travelled on one of the <u>ships</u> of the First Fleet that arrived in Australia in 1788.

Soon after the First Fleet arrived in Sydney, there were <u>problems</u>. The food they'd brought with them from England would soon be gone and Governor Phillip knew that they must grow their own <u>food</u> or they would starve.

James Ruse told Governor Phillip that he had <u>experience</u> as a farmer. He asked if he could have some <u>land</u> to grow food and show that he could become self-sufficient in a short period of time. Governor Phillip allowed James to live and work on land near the Parramatta River, twenty <u>kilometres</u> west of Sydney.

James and his <u>wife</u>, Elizabeth, were given <u>clothes,</u> tools, <u>chickens</u> and some vegetable <u>seeds</u>, as well as help to clear and dig more land. They worked hard and after only fifteen <u>months</u> they could say they were successful. They showed that it was possible for a <u>family</u> to survive through farming in the colony of New South Wales.

As a <u>reward</u> for his hard work Governor Phillip allowed James to keep the farm. This happened in 1791 and was the first land grant to a convict in <u>Australia</u>. James and Elizabeth had three children, and later sold their first <u>farm</u> and moved on to build a much bigger one. Later they had problems such as <u>droughts</u> and floods. However, they showed that hard <u>work</u> could bring success, even when other people didn't believe it was possible.

C) James Ruse - Language activities – Nouns and adjectives

The weather was <u>hot</u>.
The ground was <u>hard</u>.

nouns		adjectives	
vegetables	food	different	bigger
farmer	colony	successful	same
watches	clothes	sick	silver
tools	cows	weak	lazy
soil	convicts	unfamiliar	interested

Soon after the people of the First Fleet arrived in Sydney there were problems. The food they'd brought with them from England would soon be gone. But the land around Sydney was **_hard_** [1] and not good for growing vegetables. The weather was very <u>hot</u>[2] and many things were <u>new</u>[3] and unfamiliar. Some of the convicts were <u>sick</u> [4] and <u>weak</u> [5]. Many of them were <u>lazy</u> [6] and not <u>interested</u> [7] in trying to grow anything.

James Ruse was <u>different</u> [8]; he wanted to give it a go. He told Governor Phillip that he had experience as a farmer. He asked if he could have some land to grow food and show that he could become <u>self-sufficient</u> [9] in a <u>short</u> [10] time. Governor Phillip allowed James to live and work on a <u>small</u> [11] area of land near the Parramatta River. Governor Phillip allowed this because he saw that James Ruse was a <u>well-behaved</u> [12] convict. It was an experiment to see if it was possible to succeed in farming in a country where the seasons and the soil were <u>unfamiliar</u> [13]. James Ruse's farm was called 'Experiment Farm'.

James and Elizabeth had three children, and later sold their <u>first</u> [14] farm and moved on to build a bigger and more <u>successful</u> [15] one.

Adjectives – spelling practice

Noun groups – Answers

1) James Ruse was born on <u>a farm in England</u>.

2) James Ruse was <u>a pioneer farmer in Australia</u>.

3) He stole <u>two silver watches</u>.

4) James Ruse was <u>a well-behaved convict</u>.

5) James Ruse lived and worked on <u>a small area of land near the Parramatta River</u>.

6) In 1791, James was given <u>the first convict land grant in Australia</u>.

7) James became <u>the owner of his own piece of land</u>.

8) James later sold his first farm and built <u>a bigger and more successful one</u>.

A) Mary Reibey - Vocabulary activity

1. _____arrested_____ – caught and asked questions by police about a crime, maybe put in prison
2. _____punishment_____ - something done to a person because they did something bad
3. _____convict_____ - a person who is put in prison for doing something bad
4. _____colony_____ - a place that is ruled and controlled by a far-away country
5. _____officer_____ - a person with an important job in the army or navy
6. _____delivering_____ - taking things to a person or a place
7. _____supplies_____ - the things that people need and use to live and work
8. _____trading_____ - buying and selling between people or countries
9. _____perseverance_____ - continuing to try and do something when things are very difficult
10. _____determined_____ - wanting to do something very much and not letting anything stop you
11. _____warehouse_____ - a very large building where things are stored before they are used or sold
12. _____retired_____ - stopped working because of old age
13. _____respected_____ - approved and admired by other people for their good work

B) Mary Reibey – Comprehension activity

1) Mary was born in England in 1777.

2) When she was 13 years old, police arrested her for trying to steal a horse. When the police arrested her, she was dressed as a boy and she said her name was James Burrow.

3) She married Thomas Reibey, a young Irish officer.

4) They started a business delivering things by boat to people who lived along the river.

5) In 1807 Thomas bought a faster sailing ship for trading with the Pacific Islands, China and India,

6) Thomas died in 1811, Mary was left with seven children and a very large business to manage alone.

7) The following year, in 1812, Mary opened a new warehouse in George Street, Sydney and in 1817 she bought two more ships. During the next ten years, her business continued to grow and she built many large buildings in the business centre of Sydney.

8) Mary became one of the most successful and respected businesswomen in the early history of NSW.

9) On the $20 note you can see a picture of Mary, a ship and one of her Sydney buildings.

C) Mary Reibey – Language activities – more practice with nouns

Proper nouns: People	Places	Nationalities
Mary Reibey	Hawkesbury River	English
Thomas Reibey	Pacific Islands	Australian
James Burrow	New South Wales	Irish
	China, Sydney, England, India	

Common nouns	concrete nouns		abstract nouns
places	**people**	**things**	conditions, experiences and feelings
colony	girl	ship	perseverance
islands	convict	picture	marriage
farm	grandmother	boat	punishment
	boy children		age
	police officer		history

Mary Reibey – verbs and nouns

noun
Mary lived on a **farm**.

verb
Mary can **farm** vegetables and animals

noun
Look at Mary's **picture** on the $20.

verb
Can you **picture** life on a convict ship?

noun
Mary was arrested by the **police**.

verb
They **police** the area after rock concerts.

verb
I **work** six days each week.

noun
My **work** is very enjoyable.

noun
What is your **age**?

verb
Your skin will **age** quickly without sunscreen.

Nouns review: Mary Reibey

Mary Reibey was an English girl who was sent to Australia as a <u>convict</u> when she was only 13 <u>years</u> old. Later she became one of Sydney's most successful businesswomen.

When she was 13 years old, <u>police</u> arrested her for trying to steal a <u>horse</u>. When the police arrested her, she was dressed as a <u>boy</u> and she said her name was James Burrow. For punishment, she was sent as a convict to work for seven years in the new <u>colony</u> in Sydney, New South Wales.

She was taken to <u>Australia</u> by <u>ship</u> and when she arrived in 1792, she was given a job looking after small <u>children</u> in a home. When she was seventeen, she married Thomas Reibey. Soon they started a <u>business</u> delivering things by boat to people who lived along the <u>river</u>. In 1807 Thomas bought a larger ship for trading with the Pacific Islands, China and India, but he became sick after a trip to India in 1809.

Thomas died in 1811 and Mary was left with seven <u>children</u> and a very large <u>business</u> to manage alone. However, the next year, in 1812, Mary opened a new <u>warehouse</u> in Sydney and bought two more ships in 1817. During the next ten years, her business continued to grow and she built many large <u>buildings</u> in the business centre of Sydney.

Because of her hard <u>work</u>, Mary Reibey became one of the most successful businesswomen in the early history of New South Wales.

You can see a <u>picture</u> of Mary, a sailing <u>ship</u> and one of her Sydney <u>buildings</u> on the Australian twenty dollar note.

Map Activity

Mary was born in <u>England</u> in 1777. She was taken to <u>Australia</u> by ship in 1792. Mary and Thomas Reibey bought ships to trade with the Pacific Islands, <u>China</u> and <u>India</u>.

Mary Reibey: Adjectives ending with 'ful'

Crossword answers:

1. (down) career
2. (down) helpful
3. (down) powerful
4. (across) successful
5. (across) hopeful
6. (across) respectful
7. (across) beautiful
8. (across) skillful
9. (across) truthful
10. (across) lawful

A) John and Elizabeth Macarthur - Vocabulary activity

1. ____founders____ - people who begin a new activity or an organisation
2. ____ambitious____ - a strong feeling of wanting to be successful
3. ____in charge____ - to be in control of a job or other people
4. ____inspector____ - someone whose job is to check that things are done correctly
5. ____produce____ - food that is grown on a farm to be sold
6. ____profit____ - money that is made from selling something
7. ____experimenting____ - trying or testing a new way of doing something
8. ____enemies____ - people who hate each other and fight each other
9. ____argued____ - disagreed with another person, shouted in an angry way
10. ____troublemaking____ - making problems for other people
11. ____opportunity____ - a good situation which gives you a chance to do something
12. ____samples____ - small examples or pieces of something to show as examples
13. ____support____ - help
14. ____exporting____ – sending and selling produce to another country
15. ____expand____ - to get bigger, increase in size and number
16. ____determination____ - a strong feeling of wanting to do something very much and not letting anything stop you

B) John and Elizabeth Macarthur - Comprehension activity

1) John and Elizabeth Macarthur are remembered as the founders of the Australian wool industry.

2) John was sent to the colony as a soldier in the New South Wales Corps.

3) He was put in charge of a farming settlement at Parramatta. He was given the job of paymaster to the army and inspector of all public work in the colony, such as new buildings and roads.

4) In 1795, John and Elizabeth began experimenting with sheep farming because they thought it would make more profit than growing vegetables.

5) Elizabeth looked after their young children, as well as the farm. This included management of the house and business accounts, management of convict workers, the shearing of sheep and selling of wool, as well as the transport and buying of new sheep. She continued to improve Elizabeth Farm and produce Merino sheep with better wool.

6) While John was in England, he used the opportunity to show his samples of wool to people in the British wool industry.

7) John and Elizabeth, with the help of their sons, were soon exporting wool to England and continued to expand their business.

8) John Macarthur was a clever, ambitious man. During his time in the colony, he made a lot of enemies. He fought with his neighbours and argued with the governors of the colony.

9) They established the wool industry which continues to be important in Australia today.

C) Language activities – prepositions

John and Elizabeth Macarthur – prepositions

1) John and Elizabeth Macarthur married <u>in</u> England <u>in</u> 1788.

2) They bought Merino sheep which came <u>from</u> Spain.

3) <u>During</u> his time <u>in</u> the colony, John argued <u>with</u> the governors of the colony.

4) John was away <u>from</u> Australia <u>for</u> almost four years.

5) He showed his samples of wool <u>to</u> people <u>in</u> the British wool industry.

6) John Macarthur was allowed to return <u>to</u> the colony <u>in</u> 1817.

7) Back <u>in</u> Australia, he gave his full attention <u>to</u> developing the wool industry.

8) John and Elizabeth, <u>with</u> the help of their sons, were soon exporting wool <u>to</u> England.

A) Governor and Mrs Macquarie - Vocabulary activity

1. ____oppressed____ - stopped from having the same rights as other people, treated unfairly
2. ____reformed____ - improved, changed to an honest way of living and behaving
3. ____policy____ - an idea, plan and way of acting by the government about a situation
4. ____equality____ - a situation where people have the same rights and opportunities
5. ____a fair go____ - a fair, honest and equal way of treating people
6. ____established____ - started a new organisation, place or activity
7. ____a vision____ - a good idea or good plan for something for the future
8. ____admired____ - liked and thought of as very good
9. ____exploration____ - travel to unknown places to see what is there
10. ____social life____ - when people meet together with friends to enjoy life
11. ____neutral____ - situation when people don't argue or take sides in a competition or fight
12. ____currency____ - the system of money used by a country
13. ____advanced____ – improved, made into something better
14. ____remembrance____ - as a way of remembering a person or event

B) Governor and Mrs Macquarie - Comprehension activity

1) Lachlan Macquarie was the fifth Governor of Australia. Later, he became known as the Father of Australia.

2) In 1810 he was sent to the colony of New South Wales to become the new governor.

3) When he arrived in the colony there were many problems. The government of the colony had become weak as the military officers had become very powerful. The army officers were more interested in looking after themselves than improving the colony. They kept the convicts oppressed so they could use them as workers without paying them.

4) He believed reformed convicts should have the same rights as free people after their time of punishment ended. He believed a policy of equality should be part of Australian society.

5) They wanted to build a place to be proud of and a place to be admired by visitors from around the world.

6) Governor and Mrs Macquarie began a building program for government buildings, hospitals, schools, parks, churches, courthouses, lighthouses and factories.

7) It was part of their plan to improve the entertainment and social life of Sydney. They hoped the racecourse would be a neutral meeting place for all people - military officers, free settlers and convicts.

8) In 1813 Governor Macquarie introduced the first official currency of Australia.

9) He used Spanish dollars and had the centre cut out of each one to make two new coins.

C) Language activities - adjectives

Country or region	Nationality adjective	Give examples by writing adjectives and nouns below: Some possible answers are shown below.
Africa	African	eg. the African continent
Asia	Asian	an Asian language
Canada	Canadian	the Canadian mountains
Chile	Chilean	Chilean music
China	Chinese	Chinese food
Europe	European	a European car
Germany	German	German beer
Greece	Greek	Greek olives
India	Indian	an Indian dress
Italy	Italian	Italian shoes
Poland	Polish	Polish music
Spain	Spanish	Spanish dancing
Sweden	Swedish	a Swedish recipe
Turkey	Turkish	a Turkish person
Vietnam	Vietnamese	a Vietnamese city

Governor Macquarie - adjectives

Lachlan Macquarie was the <u>fifth</u>[1] governor of Australia. He was the son of a <u>Scottish</u> [2] farmer. During his twelve years in charge of the colony, he and Elizabeth made many <u>important</u>[3] improvements. The government of the colony had become <u>weak</u>[4] since Governor Phillip left in 1792 because the <u>military</u> [5] officers had become very <u>powerful</u>[6].

The Macquaries believed <u>reformed</u> [7] convicts should have the <u>same</u> [8] rights as <u>free</u> [9] people. They also established a school for <u>Aboriginal</u> [10] children. During Macquarie's time as governor, the <u>white</u> [11] population of Australia increased. This included a <u>large</u> [12] increase in the number of <u>new</u> [13] convicts. He organised exploration of the country beyond the <u>coastal</u> [14] area of Sydney. He ordered a road to be built across the mountains and established the first <u>inland</u> [15] city.

The Macquaries organised the first <u>official</u> [16] horse-race in Australia as part of their plan to improve the entertainment and <u>social</u> [17] life of Sydney. The racecourse was designed as a <u>neutral</u> [18] meeting place for all people.

In 1813 Macquarie introduced the first official currency of Australia. He used <u>Spanish</u> [19] dollars and had the centre cut out of each one to make two new coins. These were the 'Holey Dollar' (the <u>outer</u> [20] circle with a hole in the centre) and the 'Dump' (the <u>small</u> [21] cut-out piece). He also established Australia's first bank, and <u>postal</u> [22] service.

Lachlan Macquaire - adjective spelling practice

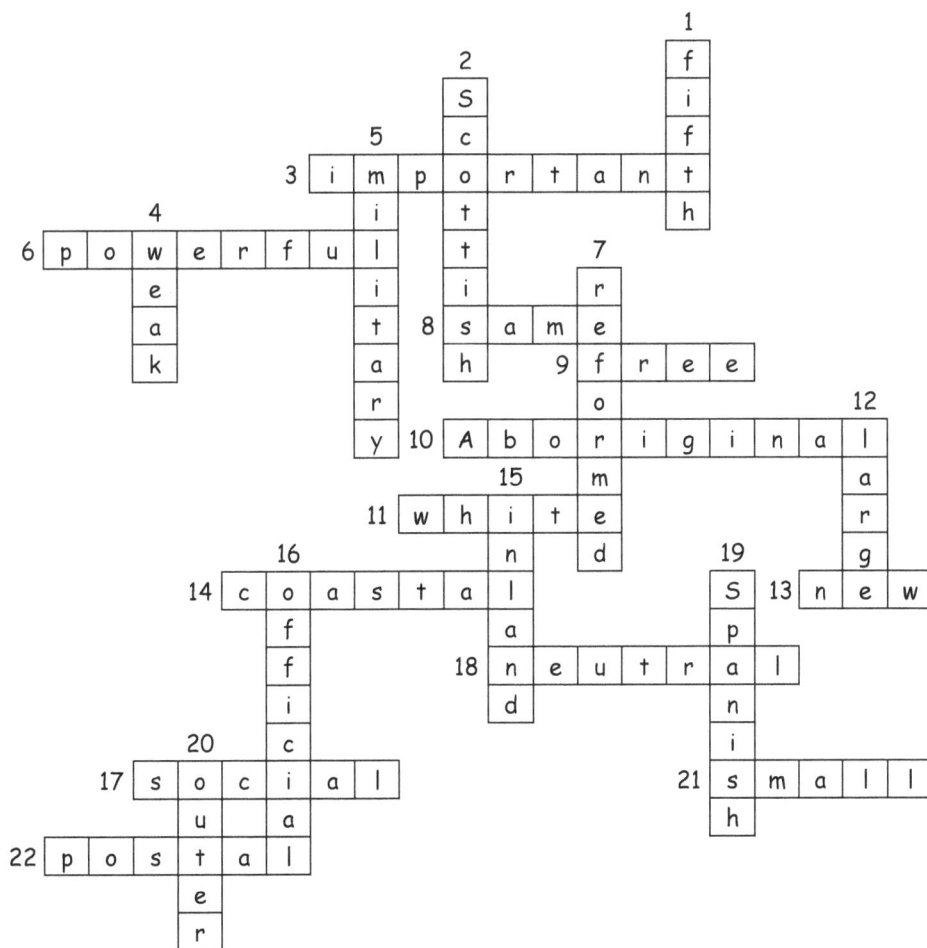

A) Caroline Chisholm - Vocabulary activity

1. ___social reformer___ - a person who works to improve the living conditions of other people
2. ___reunite___ - bring together again
3. ___stand by___ - allow something bad to happen because nothing is done to stop it
4. ___inhumane conditions___ - conditions where people are in a very bad situation
5. ___turn into___ - change to a different purpose, change to become something different
6. ___desperate___ - in a bad or serious situation with little or no hope
7. ___persistent___ - continuing to do or ask something until you get what you want
8. ___convinced___ - made another person believe that something is a good idea
9. ___employment agency___ - an organisation that helps people to find jobs
10. ___rural areas___ - places away from the towns, in the countryside, often farming areas
11. ___advertising campaign___ - activities to advertise that something new is going to happen
12. ___the bush___ - the wild parts of Australia, the rural areas where few people live
13. ___work contracts___ - agreement between employers and workers about pay and condition
14. ___benefit___ – help to improve something
15. ___outstanding___ - excellent, very special

B) Caroline Chisholm - Comprehension activity

1) Caroline Chisholm was a social reformer who improved the lives of thousands of women in early Australia.
2) Caroline was shocked to see many young homeless women sleeping on the streets. Many of these women were not convicts; they had come to Australia as free women looking for a better life.
3) Caroline asked Governor Gipps for the use of an old building as a home for the desperate young women. She convinced him that her idea would help the colony as well as the young women.
4) Caroline's next project was to organise an employment agency for the women who needed to find jobs.
5) She knew that many families in rural areas needed female workers to help look after their home and children She started an advertising campaign to find employment for the women by sending letters to wealthy farmers.
6) She went with them because many of the women were afraid to leave the city alone and were frightened of the bush. Also, she wanted to make sure they would be treated well in their new situation.
7) Within a year she had found jobs and homes for almost a thousand women.
8) She returned to England in 1846 to talk to the government about helping the husbands, wives and children of convicts to travel to Australia so that the families could be together again.
9) She accepted no money for her work.
10) Caroline is remembered as one of Australia's most outstanding women.

C) Language activities – personal pronouns

When Caroline arrived in Sydney, <u>she</u> saw many young homeless women sleeping on the streets. Many of these women were not convicts; <u>they</u> had come to Australia looking for a better life. But when <u>they</u> arrived in Sydney there were no jobs for <u>them</u> and there was nowhere for <u>them</u> to live. Caroline asked Governor Gipps for the use of an old building for <u>them</u>. At first the governor said no; <u>he</u> said <u>it</u> would cost too much money. But Caroline was persistent. She convinced <u>him</u> that her idea would help the colony. <u>She</u> worked hard to clean and prepare the old building which became a home for almost a hundred women. She called <u>it</u> the 'Female Immigrants' Home'.

Nouns with the suffix 'ment'

```
                                    1          2
                         3          r          a              4
   5                6  m a n a g e m e n t      s              s
   e                   o          t          7  s e t t l e m e n t
   q  8  i m p r o v e m e n t    i             e              a
   u                   e          r  9  d i s a g r e e m e n t
   i                   m          e             s              e
10 p  u n i s h m e n t           e  11 a m u s e m e n t       m
   m                   n          n             e              e
   e                   t          e  12 e n j o y m e n t       n
   n                              n             t              t
   t                              t
```

A) Edmund Barton - Vocabulary activity

1. _____transition_____ - when there is a change from one way of doing something to another way
2. _____separate_____ - not joined together, not related to each other
3. _____colonies_____ - countries, or parts of countries ruled by a more powerful country
4. _____nation_____ - the people of one country
5. _____continent_____ - one of the large areas of land on the earth, such as Asia, Africa, Australia
6. _____Federation_____ - a group of countries or groups of people joined together as a nation
7. _____Constitution_____ - a set of written laws that a government must follow
8. _____Commonwealth_____ - a democratic country that was under British rule in the past
9. _____lawyer_____ - a person who gives advice about the law and works in a law court
10. _____speeches_____ - formal talks given to groups of people
11. _____democracy_____ - system of government where people decide and vote for their leader
12. _____election_____ - a time when people choose or vote for a leader
13. _____court_____ - a place where decisions about laws and punishment happen
14. _____role_____ - the job that something or someone does
15. _____judge_____ - the person in court who decides the punishment of a person
16. _____contribution_____ - something that someone does to help other people or to make something successful

B) Edmund Barton - Comprehension activity

1) Edmund Barton was the first Prime Minister of Australia.
2) Edmund Barton was born in Sydney, New South Wales in 1849.
3) Before Edmund Barton became Prime Minister, there were six separate colonies in different places around the continent of Australia.
4) Barton worked very hard to develop a Constitution for the Federation of Australia.
5) Federation happened in 1901.
6)   New South Wales   Queensland   South Australia,
         Tasmania   Victoria   Western Australia.
7) The Constitution is the basis for the laws of the government of Australia.
8) The people of the Australian colonies were invited to vote to agree on the Constitution before Federation.
9) In 1903, Barton became a judge of the High Court of Australia.
10) The High Court is the most powerful court in Australia and its role is to make sure the laws of Australia's Constitution are followed correctly.

C) Edmund Barton - Language activities – punctuation: capital letters

Titles and names of people Prime Minister Edmund Barton	Titles and names of countries Commonwealth of Australia
Names of nationalities British, Australian	Name or title of an organisation High Court of Australia
Names of states New South Wales, Queensland, Victoria South Australia, Western Australia, Tasmania	Name of a city Sydney
Name of a special event Federation	Title of a book or important writing Constitution

Edmund Barton - Capital letters

Edmund Barton was born in Sydney, New South Wales in 1849. He was a very good student at school and at university. After university, he worked as a lawyer in Sydney and in 1879 he became a member of the government of the New South Wales colony.

Edmund Barton - Capital letters (continued from page 135)

Between the years of 1880 and 1900 there was a lot of discussion about the future of Australia. At that time, the six colonies around the country had their own laws and each colony had different ideas about the way things should happen. The colonies were called New South Wales, Queensland, South Australia, Tasmania, Victoria and Western Australia. People around the country started to talk about the idea of coming together as one nation instead of being six small colonies; but not everyone agreed.

When the Australian colonies joined together, Barton was asked to act as Prime Minister until an election was held. He was then elected as the first Prime Minister of the Commonwealth of Australia. At the time of Federation in 1901, the High Court of Australia was also formed. The High Court is the most powerful court in Australia and its role is to make sure the laws of Australia's Constitution are followed correctly. When Barton left the position of Prime Minister in 1903, he became a judge of the High Court of Australia.

Words with suffix 'ion'

1. action	7. progression	13. suggestion	19. revision
2. construction	8. expression	14. education	20. operation
3. constitution	9. collection	15. discussion	21. transportation
4. communication	10. federation	16. depression	22. examination
5. population	11. possession	17. invitation	23. connection
6. information	12. election	18. illustration	24. pollution

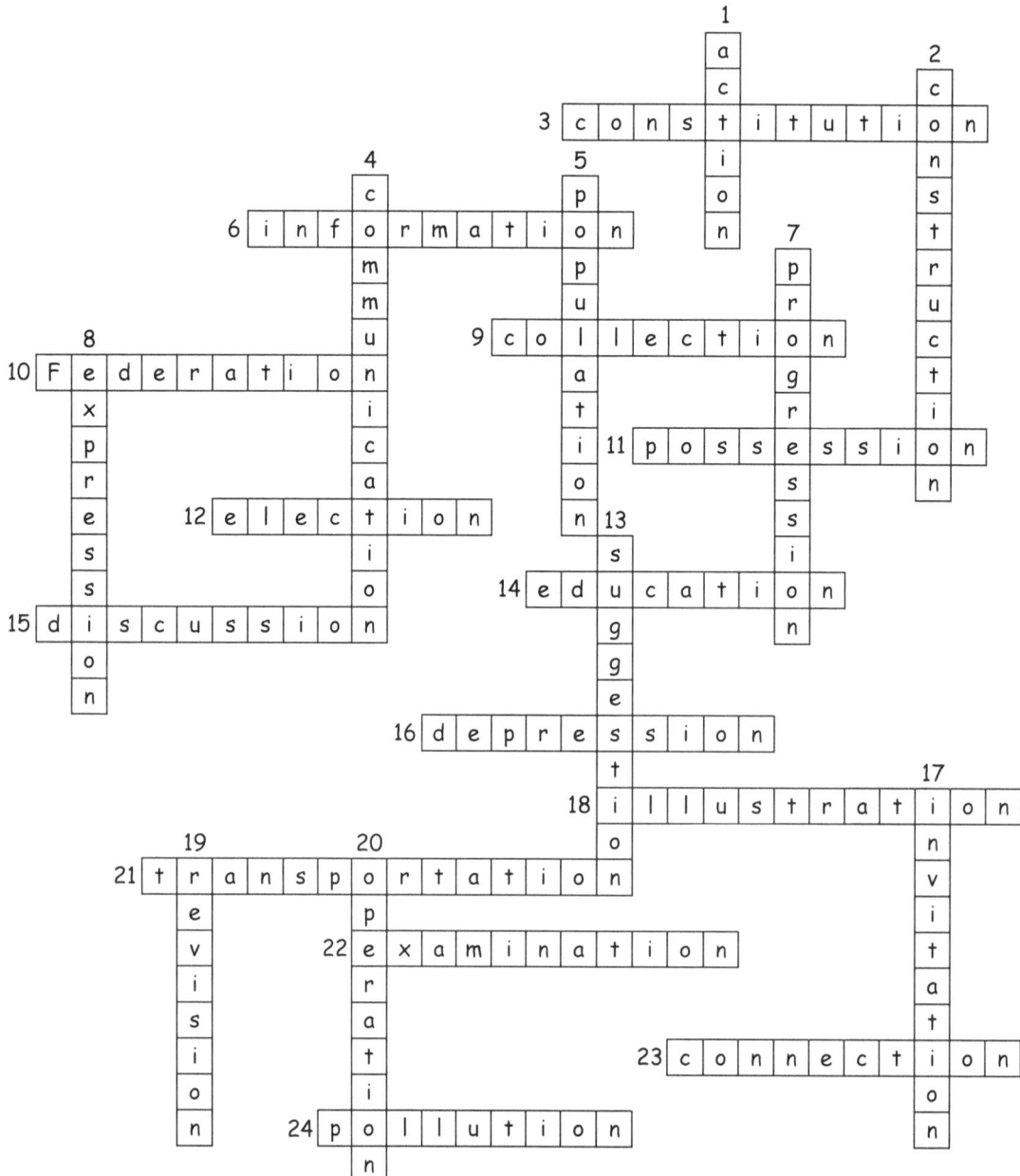

© Boyer Educational Resources

A) Edith Cowan - Vocabulary activity

1. _____elected_____ - chosen by the people for a job in the government
2. _____promoted_____ - helped something to develop; tried to make something happen
3. _____welfare_____ - health, happiness, safety and well-being
4. _____rights_____ - things that people are allowed to do and have
5. _____boarding school - a school where students live away from their family
6. _____hanged_____ - killed by hanging with a rope put around the neck
7. _____serious_____ - describing a person who is quiet, not laughing very much
8. _____court_____ - a place where decisions about laws and punishment happen
9. _____concerned_____ - worried
10. _____social issues_____ - issues about the way people live, such as health and housing
11. _____unjust_____ - unfair, not a good or right way of treatment
12. _____legal system_____ - the way of the laws in the country
13. disadvantaged groups – groups of people who don't have the same chances and help as most people in society
14. _____parliament_____ – the people who are part of the government where laws of the country are made
15. _____awarded_____ – given a special prize (award) for doing something good

B) Edith Cowan - Comprehension activity

1) Edith Cowan was the first woman to be elected to an Australian parliament.

2) Edith was born in Geraldton, in Western Australia in 1861.

3) Her mother died when she was 7 and she was sent to boarding school. Her father remarried, but was unhappy and he began to drink too much alcohol. When Edith was 15, he killed his second wife and he was hanged.

4) She became concerned with social issues and the unjust way she believed some people were treated in the legal system. She was particularly concerned about women's health and the welfare of disadvantaged groups, such as young children, unmarried mothers and migrant groups.

5) She wanted to make life better for these people through migrant welfare, baby health centres and equal rights for women.

6) In 1920, for the first time in Australia, women were allowed to compete for a position in Parliament.

7) In 1921 Edith became the first woman to be elected to an Australian parliament.

8) Her picture is on the Australian fifty dollar note.

Australian banknotes

Australia's five dollar note:

Front: Her Majesty Queen Elizabeth II   Back: Australia's Parliament House.

Australia's ten dollar note:

Front: Banjo Paterson (writer)   Back: Mary Gilmore (writer and social reformer)

Australia's twenty dollar note:

Front: Mary Reibey (convict; businesswoman)   Back: John Flynn (founder of Royal Flying Doctor Service)

Australia's fifty dollar note:

Front: David Unaipon (writer & inventor)   Back: Edith Cowan (social reformer & parliamentarian)

Australia's hundred dollar note:

Front: Dame Nellie Melba (opera singer)   Back: Sir John Monash (army officer)

Other features of Australia's banknotes can be seen at www.banknotes.rba.gov.au/banknote-features/

A) Banjo Paterson - Vocabulary activity

1. __poems__ – pieces of writing that have words that rhyme, have the same sound
2. __nickname__ – an informal name, often used by friends instead of a real name
3. __the Australian bush__ - the wild parts of Australia, away from the towns and cities
4. __coaches__ - transport pulled by horses, used to take people from one place to another place
5. __drovers__ - people who move sheep or cattle across the country
6. __lawyer__ - a person who gives advice about the law and works in a law court
7. __ballads__ - songs that tell a story
8. __published__ - printed in a book, newspaper or magazine
9. __popular__ - liked by many people
10. __voyages__ - long trips to another place by ship
11. __volunteer__ - a person who works without payment of money
12. __vet__ - a person who gives medical help to sick animals
13. __characters__ - interesting people
14. __outback__ - the wild, open inland parts of Australia, away from the cities
15. __hardships__ - problems or difficult situations
16. __pleasures__ - happiness and enjoyment

B) Banjo Paterson - Comprehension activity

1) Banjo Paterson was a famous writer. 'Waltzing Matilda' became one of Australia's best known songs.
2. No. 'Banjo' was a nickname he used when he first started writing. Banjo Paterson's real name was Andrew Barton Paterson.
3) He lived on a farm near Yass, in NSW.
4) He saw people travelling in coaches, horse riders from the Snowy Mountains and drovers on horses taking sheep and cattle across the country.
5) He worked in a lawyer's office and after a few years, he became a lawyer.
6) In 1895, he wrote the ballad, 'Walzing Matilda'
7) His stories were about characters in the Australian outback; his beautiful poems were about the hardships and the pleasures of living in the Australian bush.
8) His picture is on the Australian ten dollar note.

C) Language activities – spelling practice: plural nouns

singular noun	plural noun
a story	stories
a copy	copies

singular noun	plural noun
a person	people (also 'persons' in US)
a cow	cattle (also 'cows')

1. places
2. pages
3. families
4. horses
5. characters
6. beaches
7. copies
8. cities
9. songs
10. classes
11. people
12. countries
13. sheep
14. stories
15. years
16. glasses

Banjo Paterson - paraphrasing practice

The ballad of Waltzing Matilda tells the story of a _happy traveller_ [jolly swagman] who travels the countryside looking for work in outback Australia.

The story explains that the _traveller_ [swagman] camped by a _waterhole_ [billabong], under the shade of a _tree_ [coolibah tree]. As he waited till water in his cooking pot [billy] boiled, he sang,

'You'll come a-waltzing Matilda with me'. As he sat by his campfire, along came a sheep [jumbuck] to drink at the _waterhole_ [billabong]. He grabbed the sheep [jumbuck] and put it in his _food bag_ [tuckerbag] for later.

Just then, along came the _farmer_ [squatter] on his _expensive horse_ [thoroughbred] and three _policemen_ [troopers] on horses.

They asked him, 'Whose is that sheep [jumbuck] you've got in the _food bag_ [tuckerbag]?

The swagman didn't want the _policemen_ [troopers] to catch him so he jumped into the _waterhole_ [billabong] where he drowned. The story tells that if you pass by that billabong now, the swagman's ghost can be heard singing, 'You'll come a-waltzing Matilda with me.'

A) Nellie Melba - Vocabulary activity

1. ____classical____ - relating to music that is considered traditional rather than modern
2. ____determined____ - wanting to do something very much and not letting anything stop you
3. ____performances____ - events of singing, acting and music to entertain people
4. ____audition____ - when singers do a short performance to show their ability to get a job
5. ____operas____ - musical performances where the words of a story are sung
6. ____stage name____ - name used by an entertainer that is different to their real name
7. ____contraction____ - a word that is made shorter
8. ____radio broadcasts____ - programs sent out by radio for people to listen to
9. ____tirelessly____ - working very hard, without stopping to rest
10. ____charities____ - organisations that give help and money to people in difficult situations
11. ____farewell____ - goodbye
12. ____audiences____ - groups of people watching or listening to a performance
13. ____funeral procession____ - special ceremony when someone dies and people move slowly in a line
14. ____achiever____ - someone who is successful by working hard to reach their goal

B) Nellie Melba - Comprehension activity

1) Nellie Melba was an Australian woman who became a world famous classical singer. She was Australia's first superstar.
2) Nellie was born in Melbourne in 1861.
3) She left Queensland to begin a singing career in Melbourne.
4) A famous singing teacher advised her to choose a stage name, so she decided to use the name 'Melba' as a contraction of her hometown of Melbourne.
5) She sang for Queen Victoria of England and gave concerts for presidents, kings and queens in Europe.
6) She set a new world record by earning more for a single performance than any other musical artist in the world. In 1920 she became the first international musician to do radio broadcasts.
7) After the First World War, she was made a 'Dame of the British Empire', which was a special title she received for her charity work.
8) In 1927, on the day Canberra became Australia's capital city, she sang the national anthem at the official opening of Australia's Parliament House.
9) She was in her sixties when she gave her final concerts in London, Paris and Egypt.
10) Her picture can be seen on Australia's hundred dollar note.

Nellie Melba

C) Language activities – phrases that show time or place

Phrases of time	Phrases of place	
in 1861	to Queensland	at school
as a young woman	in Melbourne	at the Melbourne Town Hall
in 1884	to Europe	in London
at the same time	in operas	to Paris
at first	in Brussels	in Paris
in 1887	in Europe	in European cities
from that time	to Australia	
in 1902		
In that year	in London, Paris, Milan, New York and other major	
In 1920	cities throughout Australia and New Zealand	
During the war		
After the war	in the capital cities	
In 1927,	in the world	
on the day Canberra became Australia's capital city	at the official opening of Australia's Parliament House	
in 1928	in Australia	
in her sixties	in London, Paris and Egypt	
in 1931	Note: the phrase 'in the war' could be understood to refer to a time period or a place (a war zone).	

Adjectives with the suffix 'al' – crossword

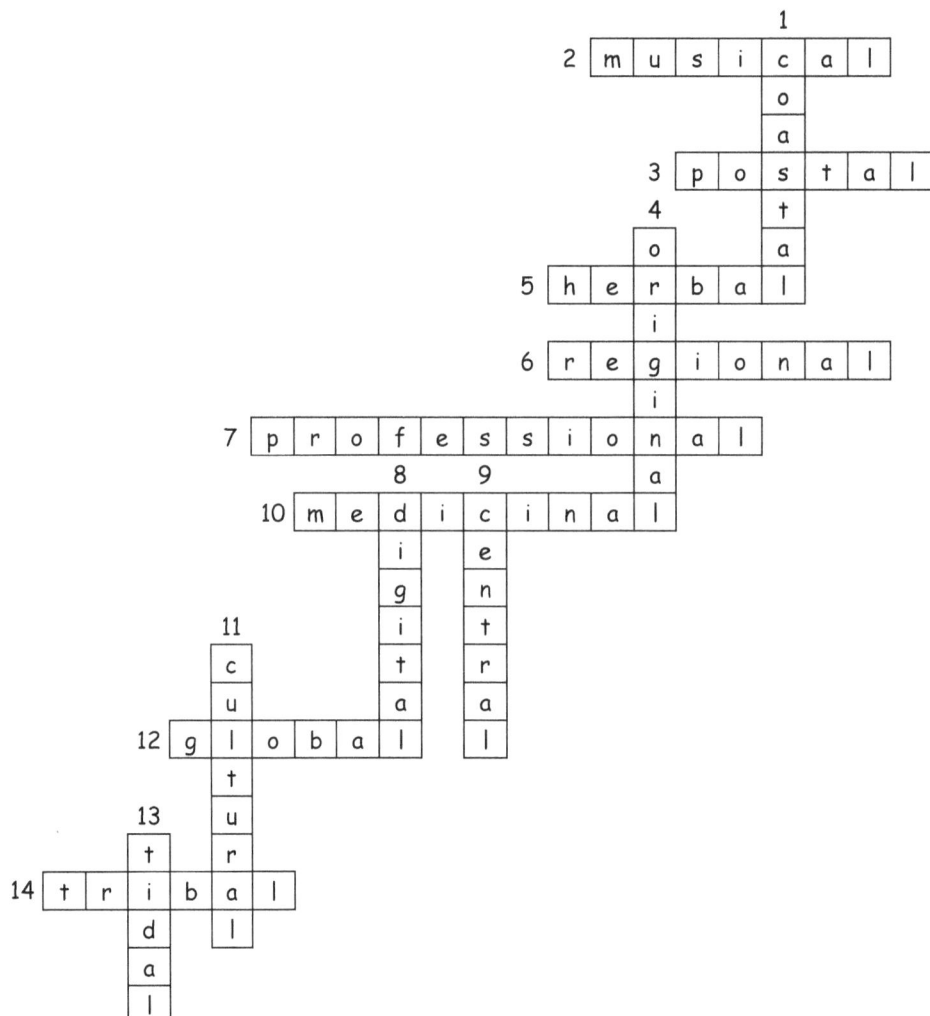

A) David Unaipon - Vocabulary activity

1. ____inventor____ - a person who thinks of new ways to make something or do something
2. ____published books____ – books that are printed and sold for other people to read
3. ____shearing sheep____ - cutting the wool from a sheep's skin with special cutters
4. ____engineering____ - planning and building bridges, roads and machines
5. ____centrifugal force____ - a force that makes things move away from the centre as it spins around
6. ____helicopter____ - a flying machine with rotors on top that turn quickly and make it fly
7. ____racism____ – when people are treated badly or unfairly because of their colour or race
8. ____legends____ – stories of a long time ago about places and people of a culture
9. ____an article____ – a short piece of writing in a newspaper or magazine
10. ____publicity____ - giving information to many people by newspapers, magazines or presentations
11. ____co-operation____ - when people work well together
12. ____equal rights____ - all people allowed to do things or have things equally
13. ____welfare____ – the health and living conditions of people in society
14. ____annually____ - happening every year
15. ____honours____ – gives respect and thanks to someone for what they have done
16. ____achievements____ – important things that a person plans and does successfully

B) David Unaipon - Comprehension activity

1) He was the first Aboriginal Australian to write published books.
2) His most famous book was about Aboriginal legends.
3) His picture is on Australia's fifty dollar note.
4) David Unaipon was born in South Australia, in 1872.
5) As a young man, he loved to read and was interested in science and music. He thought a lot about new ways to fix engineering problems.
6) David made nine important inventions, including a motor run by centrifugal force. He also made drawings for a helicopter design.
7) He got the idea from the Australian boomerang and the way it moved through the air.
8) He gave talks in schools and churches about Aboriginal legends and culture and about his people's future.
9) He also wrote about the need for co-operation between white and black people, and the need for equal rights for both black and white Australians.
10) The 'David Unaipon Award' is an award given annually to new Aboriginal writers to help get their books published. The award also honours David's achievements in writing, science and Aboriginal welfare.

C) David Unaipon - Language activities – prepositions

1) Shearers take wool off sheep.　　　2) Helicopters can fly below the clouds.
3) He was born in South Australia, in 1872.　　4) He thought a lot about science.

Using the correct preposition

1) David Unaipon was the first Aboriginal person in Australia to write published books. His most famous book was about Aboriginal legends.
2) As a young man, he loved to read and was very interested in science and music. He thought a lot about new ways to fix engineering problems.
3) David lived most of his life in Adelaide and worked for the 'Aborigines Friends' Association'.
4) He worked and travelled around south-eastern Australia for fifty years and often gave talks in schools and churches of different religions about Aboriginal legends.
5) Sometimes, while travelling from town to town, he was told he couldn't stay in a hotel because he was black, so he understood the problems of racism.
6) He also wrote about the need for co-operation between white and black people, and the need for equal rights for both black and white Australians.
7) He worked very hard to make life better for Aboriginal people.
8) In 1929, he helped with a government inquiry into Aboriginal health and welfare.
9) In 1995, David Unaipon's picture was put on the Australian $50 note, with a drawing of one of his inventions.

David Unaipon - Adverbs of frequency

1. He thought a lot about new ways to fix engineering problems.
2. He often gave talks in schools and churches of different religions about Aboriginal legends.
3. Sometimes, while travelling from town to town, he was told he couldn't stay in a hotel because he was black.
4. The 'David Unaipon Award' is an award given annually to new Aboriginal writers.

	Adverb	Meaning
1)	occasionally	happening once in a while, not regularly
2)	always	happening all the time
3)	never	happening at no time
4)	usually	happening regularly, most of the time
5)	sometimes	happening on some occasions, now and then
6)	rarely	hardly ever happening, almost never happening
7)	annually	happening every year
8)	frequently	happening often or many times
9)	quarterly	happening every three months
10)	weekly	happening every week
11)	hourly	happening every hour
12	monthly	happening every month

Adverbs of frequency – spelling practice

(crossword)

1 (down): occasional — o c c a s i o n a l l y
2 (across): always — a l w a y s
3 (down): never — n e v e r
4 (down): usually — u s u a l l y
5 (down) / (across): sometimes — s o m e t i m e s
6 (down): rarely — r a r e l y
7 (across): never — n e v e r
8 (across): frequently — f r e q u e n t l y
9 (across): quarterly — q u a r t e r l y
10 (across): weekly — w e e k l y
11 (across): hourly — h o u r l y
12 (across): monthly — m o n t h l y

A) Charles Kingsford Smith - Vocabulary activity

1) pilot – a person who flies a plane
2) record-breaking – doing or recording something better than anyone or anything else before
3) mechanics - the study of machines and how they move and work
4) cockpits - the part of a plane where pilots sit and operate the controls
5) exposed - having no cover or protection from the weather
6) amputated - cut off from the body as part of a medical operation
7) medal – a small, metal object, given as a prize for doing something special
8) courage - to be in a dangerous situation but not be afraid, to be brave
9) stunt - a dangerous act that is done to entertain people, especially in movies
10) to focus - to make something the centre of your attention
11) major - the most important or main thing
12) goal - something you want to do successfully in the future, an aim
13) contribution - something that a person gives or does to help a situation
14) aviation - everything related to flying planes and other aircraft

B) Charles Kingsford Smith - Comprehension activity

1) Kingsford Smith was a famous Australian pilot.
2) When he was thirteen, he began studying mechanics at college.
3) He joined the army and became a soldier in the First World War
4) The planes then were made of wood, fabric and wire. They were difficult and dangerous to fly and had open cockpits so the pilots were exposed to bad weather.
5) He was shot in the foot when his plane was attacked. As a result, several of his toes were amputated. This injury ended his career in the British Air Force.
6) He went to America, where he worked as a stunt pilot in Hollywood movies for several years.
7) In 1927, he completed an around-Australia flight in ten days and five hours.
8) 1928: he made the 1st flight across the Pacific Ocean from USA to Australia in the 'Southern Cross'.
   1929: He made a flight from Australia to England and set a new record of twelve days and eighteen hours.
   1930: He began his own airline, 'Australian National Airways',
9) In 1935, he disappeared while flying between India and Singapore and was never seen again.
10) His picture was on the Australian $20 note until 1994, when a new $20 note was designed. He was given the title 'Sir Charles Kingsford Smith'. 'Sydney Kingsford Smith Airport' was named after him.

C) Charles Kingsford Smith - Language activities – paragraphs

The main idea of paragraph 1 is: c) who Kingsford Smith was
The main idea of paragraph 2 is: c) Kingsford Smith's early life
The main idea of paragraph 3 is: b) Kingsford Smith's flying experiences during the war
The main idea of paragraph 4 is: a) Kingsford Smith's experience in America
The main idea of paragraph 5 is: a) Kingsford Smith's flying experiences around Australia
The main idea of paragraph 6 is: c) Kingsford Smith's flying achievements
The main idea of paragraph 7 is: a) Kingsford Smith's disappearance and how he's remembered

Past tense verbs - review

regular past tense			irregular past tense			
joined	enjoyed	disappeared	was	made	began	
compared	exposed	completed	became	were	shot	
attacked	ended	returned	sent	went	thought	
awarded	worked	named died	gave	quit	flew	set

Practice 1) Active and passive verbs

At the age of eighteen, he joined the army and became a soldier in the First World War. He was sent to fight in France, Egypt and Gallipoli. Later, he joined a new unit of the British Forces that would fly planes for the first time.

The planes then were made of wood, fabric and wire. They were difficult and dangerous to fly and had open cockpits so the pilots were exposed to bad weather.

During the war, he was shot in the foot when his plane was attacked. As a result, several of his toes were amputated. This injury ended his career in the British Air Force. He was only twenty years old but he was awarded the 'Military Cross', which was a medal to reward his courage.

His picture was on the Australian $20 note until 1994, when a new $20 note was designed. He was given the title 'Sir Charles Kingsford Smith' for his contribution to aviation. Sydney's international airport, 'Sydney Kingsford Smith Airport' was named after him.

Practice 2)

Active sentence	Passive sentence
1. The army sent Kingsford Smith to France.	Kingsford Smith was sent to France
2. Manufacturers made the first planes with wood and wire.	The first planes were made with wood and wire.
3. The open cockpits exposed the pilots to bad weather.	The pilots were exposed to bad weather.
4. The enemy attacked his plane.	His plane was attacked.
5. Doctors amputated several of Kingsford Smith's toes.	Several of Kingsford Smith's toes were amputated.
6. The army awarded Kingsford Smith a medal.	Kingsford Smith was awarded a medal.
7. The government gave him the title 'Sir Kingsford Smith'.	He was given the title 'Sir Kingsford Smith'.
8. They named Sydney's international airport after him.	Sydney's international airport was named after him

A) John Flynn – Vocabulary activity

1. _____outback_____ – places were few people live, far away from town and cities
2. _____minister_____ – a person who works for a Christian church
3. _____remote_____ – very far away from cities and city services
4. _____urgent need_____ – when help is needed as soon as possible, immediately
5. _____vast_____ – very, very large (to describe an area)
6. _____isolated communities_____ – people living far away from other people and services
7. _____set up_____ – organise an activity or the building of something
8. _____radio communication_____ – using radio to send and receive messages from other people
9. _____pedal radio_____ – making power for radio by pedalling with the feet
10. _____generator_____ – a machine that makes electricity
11. _____communication network_____ – people and places linked by radio or other ways of communication
12. _____award_____ – a prize for doing something special
13. _____QANTAS_____ – Queensland and Northern Territory Aerial Services
14. _____continent_____ – one of the earth's very large areas of land
15. _____pilot_____ – a person who flies a plane

B) John Flynn – Comprehension activity

1) John Flynn started the Flying Doctor Service of Australia.
2) In 1903 he became a Christian minister and began visiting small towns in remote areas of Australia.
3) He saw the urgent need for health care for people living in the vast Australian outback. He heard many sad stories of sick people dying before they could get to a hospital.
4) He used his magazine to make known his plans and to raise money so he could set up simple 'bush hospitals' in small outback towns to help outback communities.
5) In 1920, he wrote about his idea of having a 'flying doctor' service.
6) 1928
7) In 1929, the first 'pedal radio' was made using bicycle pedals to drive a generator and Flynn used the idea to set up a communication network for outback communities.
8) His picture is on the Australian $20 note with a picture of the QANTAS plane used by the organisation.
9) The Royal Flying Doctor Service is used across 7,000,000 square kilometres, or 80% of Australia.
10) Royal Flying Doctor Service

C) John Flynn – Language activities – Adjectives: review

> John Flynn saw the urgent need for health care for people living in the Australian outback.
> He wanted to help the isolated communities of inland Australia. In 1920, he wrote about his
> idea of having a 'flying doctor' service which was an amazing idea in those days.
>
> The service he began in 1928 continues to be the largest 'air ambulance' service in the world.
>
> Note:
> In the above sentences, the terms, 'flying doctor' and 'air ambulance' are compound nouns but here act as adjectives to describe 'service'.

Adjectives with special suffixes

1) 'ed' Find an example in the sentences in the box above about John Flynn?   _____isolated_____
2) 'ing' Find an example in the sentences above about John Flynn?   _____amazing_____
3) 'est' Find an example in the sentences about John Flynn?   _____largest_____

Abbreviations: acronyms

QANTAS = Queensland and Northern Territory Aerial Services
NAIDOC = National Aborigines and Islanders Day Observance Committee
ANZAC   = Australia and New Zealand Army Corps

Synonyms					
1. far away	remote		8. started	began
2. biggest	largest		9. immediately necessary	urgent
3. give, supply	provide		10. unhappy	sad
4. a long way	far		11. sufficient	enough
5. well known	famous		12. problems	difficulties
6. surprising	amazing		13. factual	true
7. huge, immense	vast		14. recently made	new

C) John Flynn - Language activities – synonyms

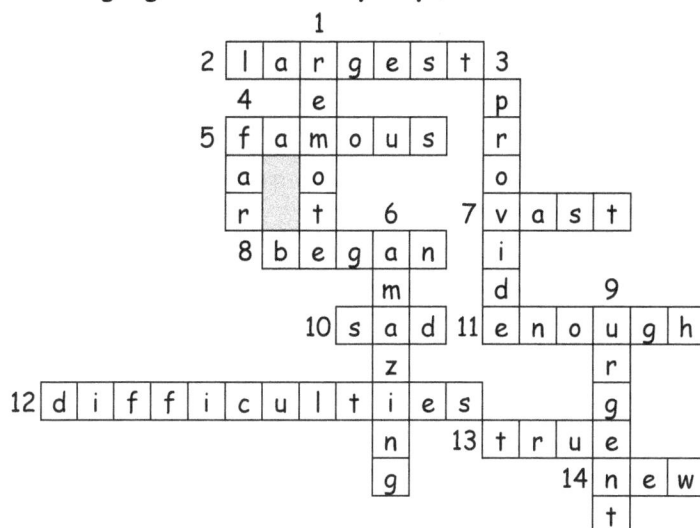

```
                        1
                2 l  a  r  g  e  s  t   3
                4     e              p
                5 f  a  m  o  u  s   r
                  a     o           o
                  r     t     6   7 v  a  s  t
                8 b  e  g  a  n     i
                     m           d        9
             10 s  a  d  11 e  n  o  u  g  h
                     z              r
     12 d  i  f  f  i  c  u  l  t  i  e  s   g
                     n       13 t  r  u  e
                     g          14 n  e  w
                                   t
```

Numerical information in the text about John Flynn.

By 1928, he had raised enough money to begin using small planes to fly doctors and nurses to emergency situations. In its first year, the service flew fifty flights, becoming the first air ambulance service in the world.

In 1929, the first 'pedal radio' was made using bicycle pedals to drive a generator and Flynn used the idea to set up a communication network for outback communities.

In 1933, he received an award called Order of the British Empire. His picture is on the Australian twenty dollar note with a picture of the first QANTAS plane used by the organisation.

Today, the Royal Flying Doctor Service is still used across 7,000,000 square kilometres, or 80% of the Australian continent. Eighty percent of medical emergencies in Australia's outback are attended by only a nurse and pilot while a doctor gives instructions to the nurse from a medical centre far away. The Royal Flying Doctor Service continues to be the largest emergency 'flying' health care service in the world.

A) Douglas Mawson - Vocabulary activity

1. ____geologist____ - a person who studies rocks and the earth's surface
2. ____explored____ - searched for new things that had not been seen or known before
3. ____contribution____ - something given to help other people or to make something successful
4. ____expedition____ - an organised trip to a place with a group of people and equipment, etc.
5. ____a base camp____ - a place where food and supplies are kept when doing trips around an area
6. ____journey____ - a trip, when you travel a long way to another place
7. __magnetic South Pole__ - the place on the Earth which a compass shows as south, opposite to north
8. ____blizzards____ - storms with snow and very strong wind
9. ____snow blindness____ - not able to see anything because of the brightness of the snow
10. ____frostbite____ - when very cold weather gives pain and damages fingers and toes
11. ____crevasses____ - very deep, long holes in ice-covered areas
12. ____sledges____ - vehicles to travel on snow, with long pieces of metal instead of wheels
13. ____chart____ - make a map or record information about something over a period of time
14. ____extreme____ - describing the most serious possible situation
15. __geological samples__ - small pieces of something (eg. rock) to study or show what it looks like
16. ____hero____ - a person who does something very brave and good

B) Douglas Mawson - Comprehension activity

1) Douglas Mawson was an adventurer and a geologist. He explored large areas of Antarctica.

2) He made one of the greatest contributions to the world's knowledge of the weather, geology and wildlife of the Antarctic continent.

3) They did scientific research in Antarctica such as scientific testing of the weather and life in the icy sea.

4) Blizzards, snow blindness and frostbite made their journey painful. They had to take care not to fall into deep ice crevasses.

5) The 'Australasian Antarctic Expedition' set off by ship to Antarctica in December 1911. They set up a communication base on Macquarie Island so the first wireless radio signals could be sent to the world from Antarctica. Then they headed to the Antarctic continent to do scientific research and chart the Antarctic coastline directly south of Australia.

6) It was one of the coldest, windiest places on the earth. Through March and April the wind speed ranged from 100 to 300 kms per hour.

7) He set out to do more exploring with sledges pulled by dogs. They travelled east for 500 kms, collecting geological samples.

8) In December while crossing ice, Ninnis fell into a deep crevasse and was never seen again.

9) After twenty-five days on the return journey, Mertz, who was exhausted and sick, also died.

10) When he returned to Australia, he was greeted as a hero and was given the title of 'Sir Douglas Mawson' for his great Antarctic exploration and research.

C) Douglas Mawson - Language activities: The use of 'articles' – a, an, the

Practice 1: In September that year, Mawson was part of <u>a team</u> that left the base camp for <u>a journey</u> of 2028 kilometres to reach the magnetic South Pole.

Practice 2: However, <u>the first radio signals</u> were successfully sent from Antarctica to Macquarie Island before <u>the tower</u> blew down.

Practice 3:

Douglas Mawson was **an** [1] adventurer and **a** [2] geologist He explored large areas of [3] Antarctica and made one of **the** [4] greatest contributions to **the** [5] world's knowledge of the weather, geology and wildlife of **the** [6] Antarctic continent.

At school, he was interested in [7] geology and later studied mining engineering at the University of Sydney. In 1905, he became a lecturer at the University of Adelaide and three years later he joined explorers on a British Antarctic Expedition to do scientific research in [8] Antarctica.

After crossing the Southern Ocean to [9] Antarctica, **the** [10] explorers set up **a** [11] base camp and began scientific testing of the weather and life in the icy sea. In September that year, Mawson was part of a team that left **the** [12] base camp for a journey of 2028 kilometres to reach **the** [13] magnetic South Pole. Mawson's team faced many dangers. After months of difficulty, they reached **the** [14] magnetic South Pole in early 1909. They took photos and raised **the** [15] British flag to claim the area for Britain. Then they pulled their sledges 2028 kms back to **the** [16] base camp.

After returning to [17] Australia, Mawson organised equipment and men for his own 'Australasian Antarctic Expedition'. **The** [18] expedition set off by ship in December 1911. Firstly, they set up a communication base on [19] Macquarie Island, 1300 kilometres south east of [20] Tasmania, so that **the** [21] first wireless radio signals could be sent to **the** [22] world from Antarctica. It took them five months to build a communication tower due to the extreme weather. However, **the** [23] first radio signals were successfully sent from Antarctica to [24] Macquarie Island before the [25] tower blew down.

Phrasal verbs - practice

1. After taking months to reach Antarctica by ship, the explorers <u>set up</u> a base camp. (set up means built)

2. The expedition **set off** by ship in December 1911.

3. Firstly, they **set up** a communication base on Macquarie Island.

4. They reached Cape Denison in January 1912 and **set up** a base camp.

5. Mawson and two other men, Mertz and Ninnis, **set out** to do more exploring with sledges pulled by dogs.

A) Vincent Lingiari - Vocabulary activity

1. <u>civil rights movement</u> - protests in 1960s to bring justice & social change
2. <u>role model</u> - a person who is admired and looked to as an example to be followed
3. <u>stockman</u> - a person whose job is to look after livestock such as cattle
4. <u>exploitation</u> - abuse and misuse of someone
5. <u>food rations</u> - fixed allowance or amount of food
6. <u>evolved</u> - developed and grew into something different
7. <u>reclaim</u> - get something back that once belonged to you
8. <u>strike</u> - a refusal to work as a protest for bad conditions
9. <u>petition</u> - a formal written request to someone in authority
10. <u>morally</u> - honestly, justly, properly, decently
11. <u>rights</u> - fair, honest and correct claims of all humans for fair treatment
12. <u>deeds</u> - a signed paper giving ownership of property or legal rights
13. <u>solemnly</u> - in a serious, respectful and sincere way

B) Vincent Lingiari - Comprehension activity

1) Lingiari was a skilled Aboriginal stockman who became a role-model in the civil rights movement.

2) Vincent Lingiari was born on a cattle station in the Northern Territory in 1919.

3) When the manager refused his people the same pay as white men, the workers left the property.

4) They asked for their land to be returned to them but the governor-general refused their request.

5) Frank Hardy published a book called 'The Unlucky Australians' bringing attention to their struggle.

6) 1972: Prime Minister, Gough Whitlam announced he would do something about their situation

   1975: the Gurindji people won their land back.

   1977: Lingiari was awarded an Order of Australia (AM) medal

7) The Gurindji people live in the <u>Northern Territory</u>, In 1883, Wave Hill Station, was set up on their land approximately 600 kilometres <u>south</u> of Darwin. In <u>1975</u> their land was returned to them.

C) Language activity – Punctuation: quotation marks

1) **A quote:** <u>'We feel that morally the land is ours and should be returned to us.'</u>

2) **A book title:** <u>'The Unlucky Australians'</u>

3) **A speech:** <u>'Vincent Lingiari, I solemnly hand to you these deeds as proof, in Australian law, that these lands belong to the Gurindji people and I put into your hands part of the earth as a sign that this land will be the possession of you and your children forever.'</u>

4) **The title of a song:** <u>'From Little Things Big Things Grow'.</u>

D) Punctuation symbols crossword

	1													

Across/Down answers:

2. capital letter
5. exclamation mark
7. apostrophe
9. question mark
11. quotation marks

Down words:
1. fullstops
4. colon
6. hyphen
8. semicolon
10. brackets
3. comma

A) Oodgeroo Noonuccal (Kath Walker) - Vocabulary activity

1. _____heritage_____ - something inherited; something belonging to a person's history or culture
2. _____injustice_____ - unfairness
3. _____racial inequality_ - different treatment because of a person's race or skin colour
4. _____domestic work_____ - house cleaning or work as a helper in someone's home
5. _____volunteered_____ - offered to do work or activity without being forced to do it
6. _civil rights movement_ - protests in 1950s to 1960s to bring justice & social change
7. _____delegation_____ - a group of people chosen to represent others
8. _____national census_____ - a count of the country's population by the government
9. _____impact_____ - an important effect or influence
10. _____lobbying_____ - trying to change or influence the decisions of government
11. _national referendum_ - a time when citizens are asked to vote on an important issue
12. _citizenship rights_ - legal rights of freedom and protection for members of a nation
13. _____Bicentenary_____ - a celebration 200 years after an important event, e.g. ~~1788~~   1988
14. _____tolerance_____ - willingness to accept ideas or beliefs different from your own
15._____creed_____ - a belief or religion

B) Oodgeroo Noonuccal - Comprehension activity

1) Oodgeroo Noonuccal (Kath Walker) was a famous Australian poet, author, and educator.

2) She was born in 1920 on Stradbroke Island, off the coast of Queensland, near Brisbane.

3) After leaving school she did domestic work in Brisbane, During World War 2, she volunteered for the Australian Women's Army Service performing various office duties.

4) She became involved in the civil rights movement

5) 1962: She met with Prime Minister Menzies, as part of a delegation, to discuss when Aboriginal people would be counted as part of Australia's national census.

   1967: National referendum when over 90% of Australians voted 'Yes' for changes to the laws for the benefit of Aboriginal people.

   1970: She received an MBE award medal for her services to Aboriginal people.

   1987: She returned her MBE medal to the government as a protest. Soon after, she changed her name to Oodgeroo Noonuccal, to express her Aboriginal heritage

6) She believed education would bring progress faster than politics, so she began an education centre.

7) She believed the biggest barrier of all between all nations, all class, colour and creed was lack of communication, lack of tolerance, and lack of understanding

8) She believed education is the answer.

C) Poetry

Note: The meaning of a word can change, depending on its context.

positive meaning	negative meaning
hope	racialism
brotherhood	ostracism
advance	ascendance
equals	dependants
freedom	exploitation
self-reliance	frustration
independence	control
education	compliance
self-respect	rebuff
	resignation

D) Language review: antonyms:

words	opposite meaning	words	opposite meaning
small	big	negative	positive
last	first	slower	faster

Adding or taking away a prefix to make the opposite meaning:

justice	injustice	unpopular	popular
equality	inequality	intolerance	tolerance

A) Oodgeroo Noonuccal (Kath Walker) continued

Adjectives with prefixes, making the opposite meaning:

1. unpopular
2. unhappy
3. unnecessary
4. uneven
5. unequal
6. unhealthy
7. untidy

8. unmarried
9. unkind
10. unsure
11. unfit
12. unclean
13. untrue
14. unwell

15. unlucky
16. inappropriate
17. dishonest
18. disobedient
19. impolite
20. uneducated
21. unfair

22. dissatisfied
23. impossible
24. insecure
25. imperfect
26. incomplete
27. incorrect
28. intolerant

Spelling – opposites crossword

A) Eddie Mabo - Vocabulary activity

1)_____spokesperson_____ – someone who represents and speaks for a group of people
2)_____ownership_____ – owning something; it belongs to you by law
3)_____centuries_____ - hundreds of years
4)_____indigenous_____ - describing the people and animals that have always lived in a place
5)_____no legal power_____ - not allowed to have control; not allowed to make laws or change laws
6)_____traditions_____ - customs; ways of doing things by a group of people for a long time
7)_____boundaries_____ - borders or lines that divide two areas of land
8)_____generation_____ - period of time from birth to the age of becoming a parent, about 25 years
9)_____a turning point_____ - a time when an important change begins in someone's life
10)_____seminars_____ - discussion classes at university
11)_____proudly_____ - happily, in a way that shows you are very pleased about something
12)_____no legal right_____ - not allowed by law to have something or do something
13)_____claimed_____ - stated or said something belongs to you; that it's your property
14)_____to challenge_____ - to say you don't agree with an idea, law or decision
15)_____without violence_____ - when nobody gets hurt or killed
16)_____court battles_____ - disagreements or arguments between groups of people in a law court
17)_____justice_____ - have good and fair treatment; fairness
18)_____won a victory_____ - showed that you were successful in a fight or competition

B) Eddie Mabo - Comprehension activity

1) Eddie Mabo was a spokesperson for Aboriginal land rights.
2) Edward Mabo was born on Murray Island, in the Torres Strait, between Australia and New Guinea, His family had lived on the islands of Torres Strait for centuries.
3) In 1879, the government decided that Murray Island would become part of Australia and would be under the control of the Queensland government.
4) It meant that the indigenous people who lived on the island had no legal power over what happened there.
5) He talked with the professors about his culture and he told them about his family's land on Murray Island.
6) They explained that the land on Murray Island belonged to the government so his family couldn't own it.
7) He decided to learn more about the situation so he could do something to change the laws he believed were wrong. He decided to challenge the idea that Australia was 'terra nullius, when the British claimed it in 1770.
8) The expression 'terra nullius' means 'no-one's land'.
9) He explained clearly how land was given from parents to their children on Murray Island. He said that the land had been stolen from his people when the government decided to take it as theirs. He said he was the rightful owner of the land owned by his father's family.
10) The court announced it was wrong to say the land was 'terra nullius' when the British arrived in 1770. The case showed that Aboriginal people could prove their right to the land they had lived on for centuries.
11) Eddie won a victory with education rather than violence.

C) Eddie Mabo - Language activities: Words and phrases that show 'ownership'

Practice 1:

1) Edward Mabo was born on Murray Island, in 1936. When he was a baby his mother died, so he lived with his uncle's family.
2) His family had lived on the islands of Torres Strait for many centuries.
3) He wanted to improve his education, so he attended seminars at the university and read library books about his people and their traditions.
4) He talked with the professors at the university about his culture and he proudly told them about his family's land on Murray Island.

Practice 2: 5) He was shocked and said, 'No way, it's not theirs, it's ours.'
6) He said the land had been stolen from his people when the government decided to take it as theirs.
7) He said he was the rightful owner of the land owned by his father's family. He believed he could win the fight for his land without violence.
8) Eddie had won a victory with education rather than violence and changed the course of Australia's history.

A) Charles Perkins - Vocabulary activity

1. _____activist_____ - someone who tries to make social or political changes
2. _____racism_____ - a belief that people of another race aren't as good as your own race
3. _discrimination_ - the bad treatment of someone due to their race, religion, age or sex
4. _____confront_____ - talk about a difficult situation with the people responsible for it
5. _____protest_____ - to say that you disagree with something that is happening
6. _public awareness_ - when people are told and know about something that is happening in society
7. _____banned_____ - when something is not allowed
8. _____hostile_____ - acting in an angry way
9. _a burning passion_ - a very strong belief and feeling about something
10. _government policies_ - a government's ideas, plans and way of acting about particular issues
11. _kidney transplant_ - an operation in which another person's kidney is put into someone's body
12. _____a fair go_____ - a fair, honest and equal way to treat all people
13. _____youth_____ - young people
14. _____champion_____ - someone who fights for better conditions and someone to be proud of

B) Charles Perkins - Comprehension activity

1) Charles Perkins was an Aboriginal activist who spent his life fighting racism and discrimination. He was the first Aboriginal Australian to complete university study.
2) Charles Perkins was born in 1936, in Alice Springs in Central Australia.
3) He played professional soccer and went to England for two years playing for several soccer teams.
4) He realised that discrimination was holding back his people in Australia.
5) Charles was one of the first Aboriginal students at the University of Sydney. While he was there, he met white students who agreed that something should be done about discrimination against Aboriginal people.
6) In 1965, Charles Perkins organised a bus trip known as the 'Freedom Ride'.
7) The students wanted to get the facts about racism against Aborigines in country towns and to raise public awareness about what was happening to Aboriginal people.
8) The stories reached national and international media, bringing awareness to the issues.
9) 1966: He graduated from the University of Sydney as the first Aboriginal Australian with a degree.
   1969: He began work as a researcher in the Office of Aboriginal Affairs.
   1972: He needed to have a kidney transplant.
   1981: He became head of the Commonwealth Department of Aboriginal Affairs.
   1987: He was made an 'Officer of the Order of Australia'.
10) Newspapers wrote 'Australia had lost a true champion'. The Charlie Perkins Children's Trust was formed in 2002 in his memory.

C) Charles Perkins – Language activities - infinitives

like	-	She <u>likes to start</u> work early.
hope	-	They <u>hope to buy</u> a house soon.
want	-	Tom <u>wants to study</u> French next year.
learn	-	You must <u>learn to spell</u> correctly.
decide	-	We <u>decided to leave</u> early.
plan	-	We <u>plan to go</u> overseas next year.
promise	-	He <u>promised to take</u> me to the movie.
try	-	I'll <u>try to finish</u> the job by 5 o'clock.
offer	-	He <u>offered to help</u> us finish the work..
begin	-	Mary <u>began to cry</u>.
continue	-	David <u>continued to study</u>.
forget	-	He <u>forgot to save</u> the document.
remember	-	<u>Remember to go</u> left at the corner.
refuse	-	He <u>refused to stop</u>.
help	-	They <u>helped to repair</u> the car.
go	-	I'll <u>go to see</u> him tomorrow.

Charles Perkins Language activities - infinitives

1) He <u>wanted to confront</u> white Australians about their treatment of Aboriginal people. (line 12)

2) They <u>decided to do</u> the same thing in Australia. (line 17)

3) The students <u>wanted to get</u> the facts about racism against Aborigines in country towns. (line 19)

4) Aboriginal people were <u>not allowed to go</u> into clubs or cinemas. (line 22)

5) By 1972 he <u>needed to have</u> a kidney transplant. (line 34)

6) He <u>continued to work</u> hard for 'a fair go' for Aboriginal Australians. (line 35)

Revision - prepositions

1) He was well known <u>for</u> his soccer skills.

2) After he left school, he played soccer professionally and went to England <u>for</u> two years to play <u>for</u> different soccer teams.

3) While he was away <u>from</u> his country he realised that discrimination was holding back his people <u>in</u> Australia.

4) He wanted to confront white Australians <u>about</u> their treatment of Aboriginal people.

5) He met white students who agreed that something should be done <u>about</u> discrimination against Aboriginal people.

6) These students knew <u>about</u> the 'Freedom Rides' in America, where students travelled around <u>in</u> buses to protest <u>about</u> racism against black Americans.

7) In one town the local council had banned Aborigines <u>from</u> using the public swimming pool.

8) In other places Aboriginal people could not go <u>into</u> clubs or cinemas.

9) From 1969 he began work <u>as</u> a researcher <u>in</u> the Office of Aboriginal Affairs.

10) Research then showed that less than 10% <u>of</u> Aboriginal children finished high school.

11) During his final years Charlie his put his energy <u>into</u> Aboriginal youth education.

Practice - pronunciation of the letter 'c'

letter 'c' pronounced as the sound /s/			letter 'c' pronounced as the sound /k/
office	cinemas	once	club
racism	decided	office	activist
central	century	December	country
places	publicity	peace	public

Crossword – spelling practice

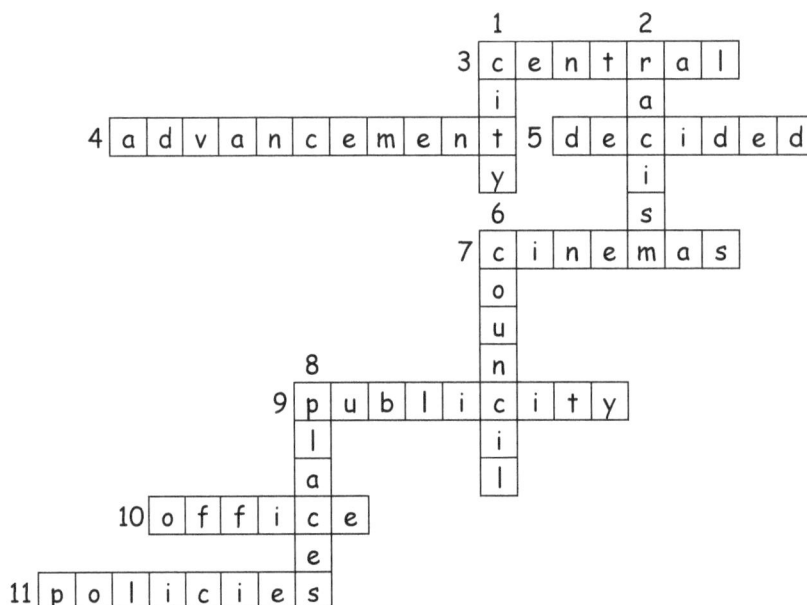

'People in Australia's Past' acknowledgements & sources:

Page 2 *Aborigine* (top) &*Two Aborigines spearing eels*, Joseph Lycett, 1817, National Library of Australia (NLA)

Page 3 *Natives in canoe,* by unknown artist, View in New Holland 2nd ed., 1824, State Library NSW

Page 7 *Aborigines spearing fish, others diving for crayfish, a party seated beside a fire cooking fish,* Joseph Lycett, 1817, National Library of Australia

Page 8 *Portrait of Captain Arthur Phillip* RN (1786) by Francis Wheatley, National Portrait Gallery, London; *Sydney Cove, Port Jackson, 1788,* William Bradley, with permission of State Library of NSW (SLNSW)

Page 9 & 21, *Chain gang* , 1808-1879 James Backhouse,,Allport Library & Museum of Fine Arts, Tasmanian Archive & Heritage Office State Library of Tasmania

Page 11 *Portrait of Captain Arthur Phillip* RN (1786) by Francis Wheatley, National Portrait Gallery, London;

Page 15, 31, 41 maps by Susan Boyer

Page 16 *Bennelong,* undated portrait, Dixson Galleries, State Library NSW

Page 26 & 30 Portrait of *Mary Reibey* as seen on Australia's $20 banknote was sourced with permission from Reserve Bank of Australia www.rba.gov.au

Page 27 *George Street from the wharf,* John Carmichael, 1829, State Library NSW (SLNSW)

Page 32 Portraits of *John Macarthur & Elizabeth Macarthur* ca.1830, State Library of NSW (SLNSW)

Page 34 *Elizabeth Farm* cottage, photographed by Len Boyer

Page 36 & 39, Portrait of *Governor Macquarie & Elizabeth Macquarie,* 1819, State Library NSW, Ref: MIN 237

Page 37 Holey dollar & the Dump, State Library of NSW

Page 38 *Convict [Hyde Park] Barrack Sydney N.S. Wales,* c. 1820 Artist unknown, State Library, NSW

Page 42 *Caroline Chisholm* portrait, National Library of Australia (nla) Ref. an9193363.

Page 43 $5 banknote issued 1967, sourced with permission from Reserve Bank of Australia www.rba.gov.au

Page 48 *Edmund Barton* PM 1901-1903: image with permission National archives of Australia: A1200, L13582B

Page 54 *Edith Cowan,* with permission Reserve Bank of Australia; & National Library of Aust (nla), Ref. an23351616. Photo: Edith Cowan Memorial, Kings Park, Perth, WA

Page 57 Banknote images reproduced with permission of Reserve Bank of Australia www.rba.gov.au

Page 58 *Banjo Paterson,* NLA Ref. an22199070; carriage: mview.museum.vic.gov.au/paimages/mm/000/PA000750

Page 62 *Waltzing Matilda* version produced by Marie Cowan, 1903; Photo of a swagman, holding a billy and carrying a swag on his back, 1901 by unknown artist (Government printer) sourced on Wikipedia

Page 64 & 65 *Nellie Melba* by Henry Walter Barnett, 1902; banknote with permission of Reserve Bank of Australia

Page 67 Statue of Dame Nellie Melba by sculptor, Peter Corlett at Waterfront City, Melbourne.

Page 70 *David Unaipon,* 1938 with permission of State Library of SA:SLSA:B7326; banknote, Reserve Bank of Australia

Page 76 *Kingsford Smith,* National Library of Australia(NLA;)

Page 77 Early aviation plane sketches by Adam Bagley; Page 79, *Southern Cross,* State Library Queensland

Page 82 & 87 *John Flynn*:, Reserve Bank of Australia; page 83, pedal wireless in SA, 1930, Australian Inland Mission

Page 88 Douglas Mawson, NLA Ref. an10932811-47; page 89, https://en.wikipedia.org/wiki/Edgeworth_David

Page90 Map, S.Boyer; page 93 Blizzard at Cape Denison: photographer, Frank Hurley 1912 SLNSW

Page 93 *Cape Denison*: https://www.flickr.com/photos/statelibraryofnsw/6433918107/ photo F. Hurley

Page 94 *Lingiari-Whitlam* image: https://commons.wikimedia.org/wiki/File:Whitlam_Lingiari_Image_3.jpg

Page 95 Gurindji stockmen near the sign to their Gurindji Cattle Station 1967, photo, Brian Manning

Page 97 Lingiari drawing by Frank Hardy: https://commons.wikimedia.org/wiki/File:Vincent_Lingiari,_1968.jpg

Page 100 Lance Corporal Kathleen (Kath) Walker, photo: c. 1942, Australian War Memorial: P01688.001

Page 102 & 103 *Aboriginal Charter of Rights,* image & poem extract by Kath Walker permission of John Wiley & Sons Aust.

Page 106 *Eddie Mabo* photo ID 1524967 with permission of Fairfax photos; page 108 map by S. Boyer

Page 110 *Charles Perkins* with permission of Monash University Archives.

Unless otherwise indicated other images are provided by Boyer Educational Resources, or obtained from Microsoft Office clipart 2003. or Wikimedia Commons public domain images.

Every care has been taken to contact and/or acknowledge copyright owners of images used herein.
For further information please contact the publisher through www.boyereducation.com.au

Further reading and research:

Australian Dictionary of Biography Online has over 10,000 biographies of significant people in Australian history.

Go to http://www.adb.online.anu.edu.au/adbonline.htm.

For more information on Aboriginal culture and history go to: www.aboriginalculture.com.au

For more information about Australia's history, government and parliament go to: http://www.peo.gov.au/

For information on Australia's democracy go to: http://www.curriculum.edu.au/cce

Boyer Educational Resources books and audio CDs

'Understanding Spoken English' – (books with audio CD) international editions

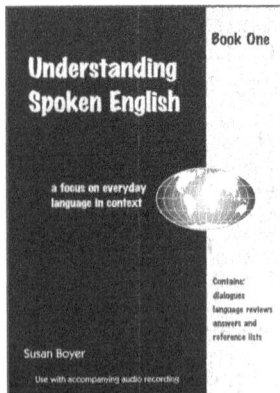

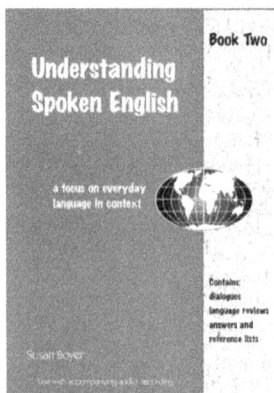

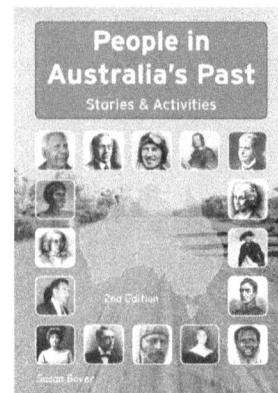

Book One

Understanding Spoken English

a focus on everyday language in context

Contains: dialogues language reviews answers and reference lists

Susan Boyer

Use with accompanying audio recording

Book Two

Understanding Spoken English

a focus on everyday language in context

Contains: dialogues language reviews answers and reference lists

Susan Boyer

Use with accompanying audio recording

Book Three

Understanding Spoken English

International edition

People in Australia's Past

Stories & Activities

2nd Edition

Susan Boyer

'Understanding Everyday Australian' – series (books with audio CD)

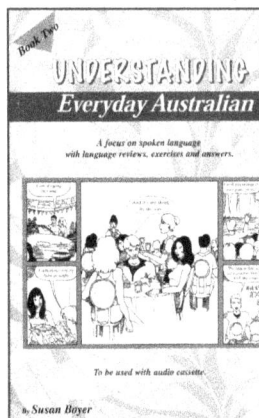

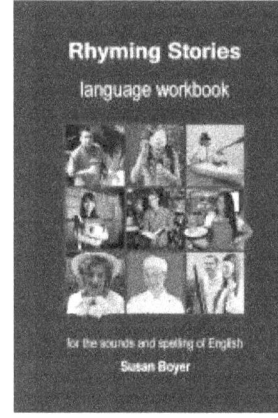

Book One

UNDERSTANDING Everyday Australian

A focus on spoken language with language reviews, exercises and answers.

To be used with audio cassette.

by Susan Boyer

Book Two

UNDERSTANDING Everyday Australian

A focus on spoken language with language reviews, exercises and answers.

To be used with audio cassette.

by Susan Boyer

Book Three

UNDERSTANDING Everyday Australian

A focus on spoken language with language reviews, exercises and answers.

To be used with audio recording

Susan Boyer

Rhyming Stories

language workbook

for the sounds and spelling of English

Susan Boyer

Spelling and Pronunciation for English Language Learners

Understanding English Pronunciation

Word Building Activities for beginners of English

English Language Skills Level One

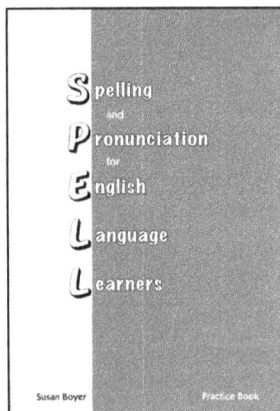

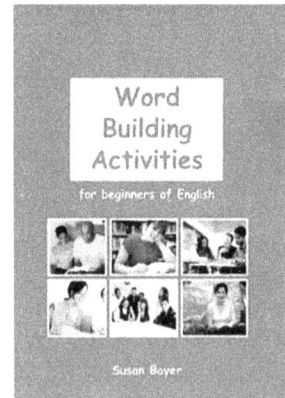

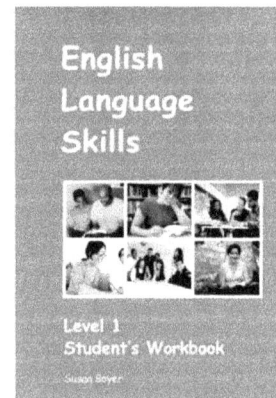

Spelling and Pronunciation for English language Learners

Susan Boyer

Practice Book

UNDERSTANDING English Pronunciation

An integrated practice course

To be used with accompanying audio recording.

by Susan Boyer

Word Building Activities

for beginners of English

Susan Boyer

English Language Skills

Level 1 Student's Workbook

Susan Boyer

Spiral bound Teacher's Books with photocopiable activities such as surveys, role-cards & vocabulary activities:

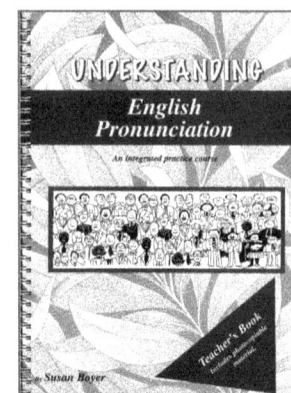

Book Two

UNDERSTANDING Everyday Australian

A focus on spoken language with communicative activities to enhance learning and promote classroom interaction.

Teacher's Book

by Susan Boyer

English Language Skills

Level 1 Teacher's Book

Susan Boyer

Understanding Spoken English

Teacher's Book Three

Teacher's photocopiable activities for classroom interaction

Susan Boyer

International edition

UNDERSTANDING English Pronunciation

An integrated practice course

Teacher's Book

by Susan Boyer

All teacher's books are A4 size. Student's books contain language exercises and answers.

www.boyereducation.com.au

www.ingramcontent.com/pod-product-compliance
Lightning Source LLC
Chambersburg PA
CBHW081136090426
42742CB00015BA/2860